The
ABC's of
Intentional Living

Dale "Bud" Brauer

ISBN 978-1-64140-892-9 (paperback)
ISBN 978-1-64140-893-6 (digital)

Christian Faith Publishing, Inc.
832 Park Avenue
Meadville, PA 16335
www.christianfaithpublishing.com

Printed in the United States of America

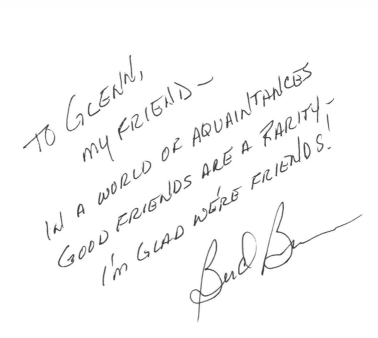

To Glenn,
   my Friend —
In a world of aquaintances
Good friends are a rarity;
   I'm glad we're friends!
      Budd B

Do you want more out of life?
Do you want your days to be more productive?

Contents

Introduction

What does it mean to live wealthy? Does it mean making lots of money? Or, perhaps, it means success in our chosen profession? Maybe it means fame or notoriety. Or perhaps, these are all empty goals, and none lead to a life filled with satisfaction and contentment. Perhaps, there's more to life and more to gaining satisfaction and contentment before our time on this earth is done. The following are tidbits of lessons life has taught; and put all together, it can lead to a more fulfilling and wealthier lifestyle, for wealth is measured in far more than money.

It is my hope that these life lessons might help you enjoy a fuller, more vibrant, abundant, and exciting life. I know they have helped me. My initial thought for sharing them was for my children, and the hope to pass along some of the wisdom life imparted to me. My daughter encouraged me to put these thoughts down in book form to pass on to others; and to her, I'm deeply grateful.

So thank you, Alisha Niccole, these are the thoughts of your father.

Always Be Conscientious

What does it mean to be conscientious? It means to be aware of that inner voice that directs us to do what is right; what is honorable; and what is good toward family, friends, or strangers. A few synonyms of conscientious are diligent, dedicated, thorough, hardworking, studious, and particular. That inner voice is our conscience, and we learn to either attune ourselves to it or learn to tune it out. The choice we make determines the bent of our moral fiber.

Those who choose to attune themselves to the whisper of their conscience find such attributes as honesty and integrity a natural outflow of their choices. Doing what is right becomes second nature, and rarely is there a battle of the conscience when life throws conflicts in our path. You're in the checkout line in the grocery store, you give the checkout person a ten-dollar bill, and they give you change for a twenty. Do you call attention to it and give back the extra ten dollars, or do you act like nothing is wrong and pocket the money? Perhaps, you stand there a moment, debating what to do, and then pick one of the above actions.

For those who give the money back, their conscience is clear, and their actions are a natural outflow of living attuned to their conscience. There is no inner battle, no question as to what to do. For those who pocket the money, likewise, have no conscience issues, not because they've done right, but because they've hardened themselves to that inner prompting to the point that they don't even hear it anymore. But those who stand in turmoil for a moment, trying to determine what to do, those are people who still recognize the call of conscience, who haven't yet hardened themselves to its call. Most of us fall into this category.

Most people like to think that we are basically good at heart, that our basic makeup is good. They like to think that, given the choice, most would choose to do what is right. While that is often the case, sadly, the opposite is also often true. Good people make poor choices. Look around, and you can't help but see example after example of our poor choices—whether it's pocketing that ten dollars, telling off the jerk who swooped in and stole the parking spot you were waiting for, deciding you are okay to drive home after a night of drinking, or tail-gating/honking at/flipping the bird at the bozo who cut you off in traffic. How about yelling at your spouse or kids, not because they did wrong, but because you had a rotten day at work and you use them as an outlet. The neighbor's dog is in your yard again, making it their personal toilet. Inconsiderate people throw trash out the car window, and it ends up in your yard. The raccoons are spreading your garbage out like a feast. So many things set us off from a slow burn to an explosion of venting. The desire to make poor choices seems to dog us every day.

Did you ever stop and consider who bears the brunt of our poor decisions? Almost always, it isn't that boss who makes your job miserable, or the unbearable neighbor who doesn't try to get along. No, it's our loved ones, those closest to us. Those who we should be honoring and holding in highest esteem. It is those we tend to unload on. We do this because these are the relationships in which we feel most secure, so we act out knowing in the end we'll still be loved and accepted. However, over time, these relationships will bear this stress only so long, and then deteriorate. (More will be covered later in "Relationships.")

Getting our moral fiber right is critical to living a successful, intentional life. We need to practice listening for that whisper that directs us to be particular in the choices we make until following that voice is second nature, automatic, and not an inner battle. The saying is, "Practice makes perfect," and nothing is truer when it comes to choosing to obey our conscience. Plus, we gain the added benefit of healthier relationships with those around us, especially our loved ones. The question is, "Why do we choose the wrong path so often, if we are basically good?"

The answer is simple, if one chooses to believe in the Bible as God's holy word. In it, we learn that, due to an act of disobedience by Adam and Eve way back in the beginning, we are all born into a world of sin. Getting our moral compass right while battling a sinful nature is a very difficult undertaking. Paul wrote of this very quandary in his letter to the Romans, saying, "For what I am doing I do not understand. For what I will to do, that I do not practice; but what I hate, that I do… For the good that I will to do, I do not do; but the evil I will not to do, that I practice. Now if I do what I will not to do, it is no longer I who do it, but sin that dwells in me. I find then a law, that evil is present with me, the one who wills to do good. For I delight in the law of God according to the inward man. But I see another law in my members, warring against the law of my mind, and bringing me into captivity to the law of sin which is in my members" (Rom. 7:15, 19–23).

If getting this right was difficult for Paul, Saint Paul, mind you, how much more so for us? But the beauty of the situation is that God provides us with a means to get this right. We'll go into greater detail in the later chapter, "Jesus." The thing to remember about God, if you are one of His children, is that He will never place you in a situation that His grace cannot keep you. And He promises, "No temptation has overtaken you except such as is common to man; but God is faithful, who will not allow you to be tempted beyond what you are able, but with the temptation will also make the way of escape, that you may be able to bear it" (1 Cor. 10:13).

What a promise! But note, while He makes the way out available, we still have to choose it. We still have to recognize and respond to our conscience, which He has provided for the development of our good moral fiber. The Holy Spirit, our emissary to the Father, speaks through our conscience. He promises to pray for us and on our behalf, even when we may not be aware. It is through our conscience that God often chooses to communicate with us.

Coveting

One of the biggest hindrances to learning to live within our own means is coveting. There is a reason that coveting made the list of Ten Commandments, the things God told His people not to do. God warned His people of those things that are destructive to living right, and coveting is very destructive. The desire for what others have, whether it is things or persons, takes our eyes off what is really important; and if we do acquire what we desire, it often turns out to be far less desirable once acquired.

A good example from my past started when I was fifteen. My dad, who was a car dealer, gave my sister a car to drive. I remember asking what car I would get when I turned sixteen, and he told me whatever kind of car I wanted because I was buying it. Well, I turned sixteen in 1974 and bought a 1966 Corvair, but not for long. Three months later, I sold it and bought a 1970 Ford Torino. A few months later, it was gone, replaced by another, and then another. In 1977, I had been through twenty cars and was driving a 1976 Ford Mustang Cobra—white with blue stripes, just like the one Farah Fawcett drove in the TV show *Charlie's Angels*. I was the envy of my class, until one night, I wrecked it. The insurance paid off the car, and I was left with a twisted mess of metal to show for my three years of working for "nicer and nicer." I realized then that every car I owned did exactly the same thing—they got me from point A to point B. It didn't matter how nice it was if it did the job, and my viewpoint changed on cars. Now, I drive a car until I wear it out, literally. My car now is a 2005 Ford Taurus bought in 2007 with twenty-two thousand miles. Now, it has over 175,000 miles, has been between

Illinois and Florida some fifteen times, and still going. And I'm still happy with it.

When we have our eyes on what others have, we cannot focus on what is really important in our own lives. Rarely what others have is important to our lives. They are wants; and if we examine things we currently have in our lives, things we wanted versus things we needed, we find the things we needed are valued and important while the things we wanted tend to end up in the corner, unused. The secret to overcoming coveting is learning to curb desire.

Curbing desire is nothing more than intentionally deciding that you are not going to give in to desire. That's it. It is developing the ability to choose wisely and then doing it. Start small. It doesn't matter if it's an impulse buy in a store or wanting a bowl of ice cream at eleven o'clock at night when you're trying to diet, it's about making the wise choice and sticking to it. You will find that, as you make good decisions, you'll feel better about yourself, and your choices and future larger choices become easier. Becoming intentional defeats coveting.

Don't Ever Forget

I f there's anything that we can all agree on, it's that life has gotten faster, and our world has gotten smaller with the advent of technology. There is a casualty of this new, fast-paced lifestyle, and that is our "families." In my lifetime, I have watched the family shrink from an extended base that included aunts, uncles, cousins, and grandparents to a nuclear base of mom, dad, and the kids. Extended family is more rarely included, save for holidays or special occasions. Everyone is connected via technology, so the need for interpersonal interaction (while needed more than ever) is mostly ignored.

As a child during summer vacation, I'd get up in the morning and go out to play. Yes, outside, and all day! Whoever's house we happened to be at around lunch, that mother would give us a sandwich and drink, and we were off again. We would play until the streetlights came on, and that, along with the calls from different moms for dinner, was our signal to head for home. We didn't worry about crime, abductions, or any of the myriads of issues we face today. There were no cell phones or pagers. If you were needed, your mom called out the back door or sent a message via a neighborhood kid. We had phones, but they hung on the wall or sat on an end table, and they were rotary dial. I remember the first push button phones—we no longer hated dialing numbers with nines and zeroes! I remember sleepovers at my cousins—many times—and at grandma's house, vacation at the lake with extended family, and family reunions on both parents sides that went back three and four generations. I remember traveling as families with aunts and uncles and cousins. They are all rich and wonderful memories. I wonder what memories our kids today will have of their family lives.

A recent study found that people averaged 280 minutes a day in 2016 on their electronic devices (phones, tablets, etc.). That is over four and a half hours a day average! The social media has replaced real life relationship interaction to a large degree, and the loss of that personal interaction is devastating on relationships. I can honestly say that one of the most important keys to a wealthy life is good, solid, foundational family relationships, and the deeper one can develop into the extended family the greater the reward. Money doesn't make you wealthy, memories do.

There have been countless cases of men who have worked their entire lives—sixty, seventy, eighty hours a week—to give their family "everything," or so they thought. All of a sudden, they find themselves in a divorce situation wondering what happened. In their mind, they gave their spouse (and kids) a nice house, cars, toys, and everything, and now they're being cut loose. They don't understand, but the reality is their family could have used less "things" and more personal time with dad or hubby.

All the things in the world can't replace a personal relationship with someone you love. And the thing to remember is it is *never* too late to work on correcting relational mistakes. It is never a mistake to try and make amends. One of the most difficult things for a man to say, especially a proud man, is, "I'm sorry. I was wrong." And yet, there's nothing that heals a rift faster than a heartfelt apology and the desire to change. Take note of this, if you are a workaholic (for it bears repeating), money cannot buy happiness, nor will it fill that void in your heart once you lose your family through divorce or whatever. Memories are what keep your soul warm as you grow old, and lack of familial memories will leave you bankrupt.

However, families extend beyond our bloodlines. We have work families—those people we spend time with and interact with on a daily basis. These relationships are extremely important too because they are our support network for a large part of our day, our week, and our life. Can you imagine trying to work at a job where no one liked you, spoke to you, or interacted with you at all? Needless to say, you would not remain in such an environment very long. We need the support and interaction from our work families. Likewise, we need to be aware and reciprocate our support to our workmates.

I remember once, as manager of the business I was to later own, I took the owner aside and told him that when he saw something done well, compliment that employee. It was a huge morale booster and would encourage them to be even more productive. Later that afternoon, as he was passing through the showrooms, the owner stopped, singled me out, and complimented me on the job I was doing. Later, in private, I had to explain again that I didn't need the compliment; those under me did. They needed to know that they were appreciated from the top down. As a manager, and later an owner, it was a practice I continued, especially during job reviews, when the boss tends to be most critical. I made sure that I always complimented something about each employee before critically critiquing their performance. Appreciation builds loyalty.

Likewise, we need to develop social families and more than electronic ones like social medias. I have developed relationships at church and in my neighborhood, and they make up much of my social family. Friends are part of our social family and, to a lesser degree, acquaintances. Everyone should have at least two or three "best friends" in their lifetime—someone you can go to with anything without fear of being judged or ridiculed, and someone you can count on as an accountability partner. But these friendships are rare, for they take time and effort to develop, and they take effort to maintain through the years. Personally, I had several best friends growing up; one was a cousin of mine, one a friend from grade school years through high school. I thought both relationships would last forever; but today, neither plays an active role in my life. Something happened in my relationship with my friend that, to this day, I don't know or understand. My cousin and I just grew busy with life and drifted apart. Busyness is the death knell to relationships.

Busyness affects us all. We tend to get caught up in the day-to-day minutia and forget about the big picture. I remember when I started in business, my boss asked for my projections on where I thought we would be in a year and five years. That is our mind-set today, we set our eyes on our future goal and work ourselves toward it, all the while forgetting that life isn't in meeting our goals, it's in the journey getting there. Life is what is happening while we're planning what we'll do next. And it passes us right by. Life is in the journey. I've been in Florida part or full-time for three years at this writing; and I've planted, raised, or seen dozens and dozens of elephant ear plants, yet recently, I was out walking in my yard and found one that had flowered! I had never seen an elephant ear plant that flowered, and it was beautiful! And yet, as I admired it and took it's picture for posterity, I couldn't help but wonder how many other plants had flowered, and I missed it because I was too busy. Life is in the journey. We must take time to slow down and smell the roses, to appreciate their beauty, and make memories. When you're old, no amount of money will warm your soul and fill the void like memories can.

We were created as social beings to be in community with God first and then others. We need relationships. We need families. Our souls long to fill that void that was created by sin and separation from God, for it was, and is, our souls' purpose to live in community with our Heavenly Father and with each other. We'll cover more on relational foundations later in "Relationships," including our most important relationship that we could ever develop our relationship with God.

As a post script to my comment on my best friend from high school, during the writing of this book, I received a Facebook message from his wife (because he doesn't do Facebook, which I sometimes envy), and my friend and I have exchanged emails and several phone calls since, catching up on life, and sharing plans for our futures. God always knows what we need, and His timing is never wrong!

Forgive and Forget?

F orgiveness is so important for successful living, for the results of forgiveness are as important to the forgiver as it is to the one forgiven. When we choose not to forgive someone for a wrong, it may affect that person to some degree, but it most definitely affects us. Holding on to wrongs or perceived wrongs is like drinking bile, or poison, and expecting it not to affect us. It will tear us up, harden our hearts, and ultimately affect other relationships because we cannot effectively compartmentalize our emotions. The bile will eventually spill over into other areas, other relationships in our lives. When we choose to forgive, we are choosing to release that bile and purge our system of it. The saying is, "Forgive and Forget." I think it would be better advised to forgive, but don't forget.

We shouldn't forget the wrongs done to us or the wrongs we have done. But we should forgive and seek forgiveness for those wrongs. After that, the wrong should be treated like a corpse; a dead person that is buried and gone. That forgiven wrong isn't something to be brought up at a later date to be used in an argument, just as we wouldn't dig up a corpse when we recall a memory of them, rather both should remain buried. We don't forget the dead person, but we don't dig them up for any reason whatsoever.

How neat would it be if we treated wrongs this way? Instead of holding on to them or bringing them up in anger during an argument, we leave them buried, forgiven but not forgotten, so we can learn from them and be relationally better in the future. Leaving them buried, but remembered, gives us a resource to be better people because we remember and can learn from our mistakes.

Something that has helped me through the years, as I dealt with negative memories concerning someone I may have had an issue with, was to try to remember a couple of good memories about them and "sandwich" the negative memory between them. Over time, the sting of those memories fade, and those good memories help me remember the good that I experienced with that person or relationship. I find I prefer good memories to hang on to.

Gotta Haves

There has been a fundamental shift in our society from my grandparents' day to today concerning gratification. It started in my parents' generation, or became more prevalent at the least, and my generation bought into it lock, stock, and barrel. I call it the "Gotta Haves," or the desire for instant gratification. Technology is moving so fast that the latest computer, tablet, phone, or gizmo today is outdated in six months. Your cell phone is now a "smart phone" and does everything from making and answering calls to be our dictionary, social calendar, alarm clock, and computer. Your watch now tells you the time, your heart rate, number of steps you take, and sleep patterns. Advertisements for the next generation; the newest models flood our airwaves. And we buy, whether or not we can really afford it, because we want, and we have credit. Back in the day, if my grandpa didn't have the money to buy something he didn't need, he saved enough to afford it. Today, we are encouraged to buy it now and pay later. And this mentality is sinking our families, our communities, and even our country.

In 1964, every dollar we printed we backed with a dollars' worth of gold or silver. Clearly printed on our currency was that it was redeemable for gold or silver or lawful currency. But then President John F Kennedy sent our Secretary of State, Henry Kissinger, to OPEC, the oil-producing Arab nations, to broker a deal in which the United States agreed to purchase certain amounts of oil from OPEC; and in return, OPEC would sell oil to the rest of the world in American dollars. Kennedy figured that having to buy oil in US dollars would keep our currency strong, and so he removed us from what was then called the "Gold Standard." After 1964, we no longer backed our money with gold or silver; rather, it was backed by oil. In reality, as we and others bought oil, our dollar became backed by our debt. We owed so much that others had to accept our currency because it was our standard to pay that debt. Today, we approach national deficits of twenty trillion dollars. Most people can't even wrap their mind around that figure. Think of a million dollars—more than most will ever see in their lifetime—and our debt is twenty million millions. That's about sixty-five thousand dollars of debt for every man, woman, and child in America.

Over the last several generations, Americans have moved from buying what they can afford to an instant gratification mentality. Credit is easier and easier to come by, and we just keep using it. My dad was a holdover from the old days; if he didn't have the cash, he didn't buy it. I remember taking a vacation to Florida one year, some twenty five years ago, and Dad wanted to go to a Federal auction being advertised, selling off seized autos and goods from drug busts. We went in and registered, and the official there said we had to use a credit card for our bidding. Well, Dad never used credit cards and only had one for emergencies with a five hundred-dollar limit, which would be the maximum he could bid. The officer wouldn't listen to the fact that Dad had thousands in his checking account—it was credit card or nothing.

I pulled out a credit card and offered it to Dad (we're the same name, I'm just a Jr.) and told him it had a twenty-thousand-dollar limit. The officer okayed it, but I remember Dad being somewhat incredulous, asking what I was doing with a card with that kind of limit? I told him I used the card, paid it off each month, and they kept raising my limit. It didn't matter that I couldn't afford twenty thousand dollars of debt; the company encouraged its use because they made their money off of debt. I was blessed to be raised by parents who encouraged responsible stewardship of my monies.

We don't find that today, however. I see young people today who can't afford to pay their rent or school loans but walk around in a six-hundred-dollar pair of Air Jordan shoes, who somehow managed to get the latest Xbox and iPhone. Personal debt is out of control. I read a recent study that claimed Americans average sixteen thousand dollars of credit card debt. That is instant gratification debt. Credit card debt is one of the highest interest rates of debt we can owe, with the exception of those "title loans" debt. I sold life insurance part-time back in the early 1980s, and we were taught then that 5 percent of the population will actually have a plan to save for the future. The other 95 percent don't plan to fail, they just fail to plan. With the rising debt we see today, I would not be surprised to see that percentage of savers even lower.

So how do we combat the "Gotta Haves?" The answer is simplistic yet difficult to implement, for it flies in the face of this instant gratification culture. The answer is to live within your means. Quite simply, you pay your bills and obligations; and if there's money left, you can buy those "extra" things. Learning to budget and then live within that budget is perhaps one of the hardest yet most fiscally rewarding things we can do. The following is a sample budget:

What is your monthly income? Gross _____ Net_____
Do you have any other income streams?
If yes, what monthly amount?   _____
Total Net Monthly income   _____

Essential/Fixed Expenses (monthly)
Mortgage/rent   _____
Car Payment   _____
Credit card payments   _____
   (Total owed on credit cards _____)
Child support payments   _____
Student loan payments   _____
Utilities (water, electric, gas)   _____
Auto insurance   _____
Homeowner or renter insurance   _____

Health insurance   _____

Medications   _____

Tithe   _____

Groceries   _____

Child-care expense   _____

Telephone (cell, home)   _____

Nonessential or Variable Expenses

Television/cable   _____

Restaurants/carry-out meals   _____

Alcohol   _____

Tobacco/cigarettes   _____

Internet   _____

Hobbies   _____

Repair/maintenance   _____

Clothing/footwear   _____

Incidentals/personal products   _____

Savings   _____

Vacation expense   _____

Misc. _____   _____

Total Expenses   _____

Net Monthly Savings/Loss

(Net income minus total expenses)   _____

Filling out a budget accomplishes several objectives. We become aware of where our money is going. Often, we aren't aware of this until we see it in black and white. If we are running a deficit, it allows us to see how far out of balance we are. Often, when living paycheck to paycheck and paying on the most pressing bills each check, we don't realize just how far off we are to balancing our budget. Seeing it on paper allows us to best determine where we can make cuts or adjustments to bring our totals in line. As an example, one place I felt was an extravagant expense in my life was cable TV.

When I had it years ago, the cost was about ninety dollars a month for TV and internet. I realized that most my viewing was network TV and that aired free with an antenna. So I cancelled my cable, kept the internet at a cost of about thirty-five dollars, and saved fifty-five dollars a month. One of my sons complained not too long ago how much his cable bundle kept going up—his TV and internet was over 170 dollars a month now. I shared what I did, and he did one better. He cancelled cable, kept his internet, and bought a Sling TV package for about twenty-five dollars a month. He was getting lots of extra stations and pocketing about a hundred dollars in savings! There are always ways to trim a budget, to work toward living within your means.

Once we learn to be fiscally responsible, balance our monthly budget, and trim back on those excesses that we sometimes don't even realize we spend, we begin to experience a degree of financial security. We find our credit worthiness rising, and this helps when needing to borrow for large-scale purchases like buying a home. It is important to get our credit worthiness in order first before any large purchase, because it will save us literally thousands of dollars in interest on major purchases. Here's the reason why. Lending institutions lend based on risk. The better your credit score, the more likely you are to repay your loan; therefore, the lower the risk. Consequentially, because you are a good risk, the lender will offer a lower interest rate because they want your business. Conversely, if your credit score is lower, it indicates that you are a higher risk to pay back your loan; therefore, the lender will increase the interest rate on the loan to cover their added risk. Acting to secure a loan before your credit is ready can, therefore, cost you thousands in extra interest.

Another question I'm often asked is how can I increase my credit score? There are several things you can do to help yourself. First, be sure to pay all your bills on or before their due dates. Lenders report to credit agencies on promptness of payment. Second, you want to pay off your highest interest rate loans first. Make minimum payments on lower interest rate loans, and pay extra on the highest interest rate loan until it is paid off. Then start on the next one, and do the same until it is paid off and so on. Once you get your credit cards paid off (which are usually the highest interest rate loans), do not exceed more than 10 percent of your total credit line in charges. Preferably, after your credit cards are paid down, pay off all credit cards monthly. Keeping your charges below ten percent of your total available credit and paying off your cards in full each month will raise your credit scores the quickest.

The bottom line is defeating the "Gotta Haves" takes discipline. It means being willing to balance your budget and commit to living within your means. It isn't easy at first, but with discipline, living within your means becomes habit forming, and then it becomes second nature. Practice does indeed make perfect!

Intentional Living

One of the most important aspects of life is mastering the art of intentional living. Intentional, by definition, means to do something purposefully. Every decision, every day, we choose whether or not we are going to be productive. Often, we make those decisions subconsciously, but not consciously weighing the import of our decisions. Until we determine to consciously choose our daily decisions, we risk just coasting through our days without accomplishing our potential. By failing to meet our potential, we are robbing ourselves of the satisfaction of accomplishment. There is nothing more satisfying than the tiredness of a job well done at the end of our day.

In the early 1980s, I went to work for the company I was to later own. Shortly after I started there, I was approached by one of the longtime employees. He told me that I was working too hard and needed to ease up because I was making the other employees look bad. I responded that it didn't matter if I was paid two dollars an hour, twenty dollars an hour, or two hundred dollars an hour, I give my best to the job. He said that we weren't paid enough to work that hard; and if our boss wanted more work from us, he needed to pay us more. We had two different mind-sets with two differing purposeful intentions, but which was right? In this example, the intentional choice to do less than his best resulted in that employee leaving within the year, opting for a factory job where he was paid by piecework, or being rewarded for exactly the amount of work he was willing to give. Conversely, the intentional choice of giving my best despite my compensation resulted in promotion and recognition, and the ultimate opportunity to become my own boss through the purchase of the company.

So how do we learn to live intentionally, to consciously choose our best option in each and every decision? Living intentionally doesn't just happen; you need to develop a plan and then implement it. It isn't enough to just want to do it. Your desire must be followed by action. In my early working days, I happened to read a book by Steve Douglas, president of Campus Crusade for Christ, called, *Managing Yourself, How to Achieve Your Potential and Enjoy Life*; and about the same time, I heard a series of messages by motivational speaker, Tony Robbins. Both carried the same theme—learning the art of time management. We are all given the same 168 hours each week; and after those used in eating, sleeping, and essentials to living, what we do with the remaining hours will determine our success in life. I took aspects from both sources and developed a daily plan to help me learn to live intentionally, one I still implement even now in my retirement.

Each night, or at the end of my workday when I was working, I would make a list of things I would ideally like to accomplish the next day. My list was usually much longer than I could realistically hope to finish. I would prioritize the list in order of importance. The following morning, I would begin to work on the first thing on my list, and I would continue until it was finished. If something interrupted me, I would get back to my task as soon as possible until the task was finished. I would then begin to work on task number two and continue to work on it until it was complete. Then I would start task three and so on until my day was over (which usually happened) or my list was done. At the end of my day, I reviewed my list; and wherever I stopped, that became number one for the following day. I would then add new things to the list and prioritize them again. I was learning to be intentional in my work.

I remember those early days when it was common for me to get only two or three items done on my list. Often, I would find myself "putting out fires" or dealing with other issues or employees during the course of my day. Yet as I became more intentional, I found myself finishing more and more items each day. I began to write longer lists, accomplishing much more than I dreamed possible. I even began writing lists at home, extending my intentionality to my off work hours. I found it also beneficial to add to those lists things like take a two-hour break, watch a movie, or take an hour break and read. I reached the point that even my relaxation times were intentional. Now I'm retired, and time restraints aren't as pressing, but I still get the most satisfaction out of my days that I've listed out and worked on. Things get done, and I feel satisfied that I am productive. There's no better feeling than the tiredness of a job well done.

As Christians, we are encouraged to live intentionally also, or designed living, as defined by Jesus's example. Conversely, those who fail to live as the Bible instructs end up default living; just going day-to-day without experiencing the purpose or rewards one gets by living obediently to God. It is our responsibility to choose correctly. Be aware that Satan prefers you and me to live in a default mode and will do whatever he can to discourage us in our Christian walk. Stand firm and be intentional.

If you want to experience a fuller, more rewarding life, then learning to live intentionally is imperative. Maximizing our time, in all areas of our lives, gives us greater satisfaction, greater freedom, greater spiritual reward, and greater relaxation than we could ever experience otherwise. There is no set right way to learn to live intentionally. I shared my way in the hopes it will help you develop your own way, your own style. Living intentionally is a cornerstone to that wealthier, more abundant life that Jesus promises us.

Jesus—A Way of Life

Christianity is often referred to as a world religion, yet that isn't an accurate description at all. Religions of the world all have this in common—each is man's attempt to connect with God. Christianity, however, is God connecting with us. Let's look at religions first.

Many people believe there are many paths to God and that to claim one is right over another is wrong. We're a brotherhood, the family of man, and all paths lead to the same end. As far as religions go that is true if we believe in the authenticity of the Bible as God's inspired word. From early times, after the fall of Adam and Eve from God's grace, man has attempted to reach God. However, the gulf separating us is too great, and we cannot overcome it no matter how hard we try. We cannot act good enough or sacrifice anything worthy enough to reach God. Despite what religions may teach, man cannot bridge the gap to God. So why do religions flourish?

Man was initially created as caretaker of God's creation, given dominion over land, sea, and air. But more than that, he was placed in Eden, God's perfect garden, to live in community with God. We were created, man and woman, in God's image, to fellowship with Him. After Adam and Eve disobeyed God and sin entered the world, our relational status changed. We were separated from our creator, but more so, we were separated from the community we were designed for. We lost the very purpose we were created for. Since that time, man has sought to fill that void that our lost community left. He has shouldered the responsibility of reaching out to God to bridge that gulf. Yet, despite what many religions teach, there is only one way to repair that gulf. I'm not going to compare here all the different avenues that try—be it Hinduism, Shintoism, Islam, Catholicism, Buddhism—the list goes on, and they all fall short because man cannot reach God. Religion boils down to dos and don'ts, lists of rules to try and please God, and we cannot. So how is Christianity different?

Jesus said, "Enter by the narrow gate; for wide is the gate and broad is the way that leads to destruction, and there are many who go in by it. Because narrow is the gate and difficult is the way which leads to life, and there are few who find it" (Matt. 7:14). What he means here is that the way to reconciliation with the Father (God) is limited, and those teaching otherwise are the wide path to your destruction. So how does God bridge the gap? He did it by sending His son, Jesus, to be born into this sinful world, live as our example, and then die on the cross to pay the price for our sins. You see, God is a just God, but He's also a merciful God, and under His justice, death is the price for disobedience, or sin. Yet, because he loves us, He sacrificed His only son to bear the sins of the world—your sin and mine—so that we could restore fellowship with Him. He tells us that if we confess our sins, acknowledge what Jesus did for us on the cross, and accept him as our Savior and Lord, we will be saved. That's it. Confess we're sinners, ask Him into our heart and life, and we're saved. It's a gift, and it's free if we'll accept it. This is the only way to restore that purpose our heart desires that we lost with Adam and Eve.

The fact that salvation is a free gift is probably the biggest stumbling block for many people accepting Him. If we reach the point where we acknowledge we're wrong, then it seems only right that we should pay some sort of penance for our wrong—that's what many religions teach. You must pay for your sins. But Jesus paid your price, so all you need to do is accept, and that's what hangs people up. It's like it's too good to be true, but it's not. It's right from Jesus's mouth to our hearts. And that's the difference that sets Christianity apart. Christianity isn't a religion then as much as it is a lifestyle choice. Jesus showed us how to live, taught us how to pray, and much in

His example flew in the face of religious leaders of his day. And the price He paid to redeem us—being separated from His father while bearing our sin—showed the endless love He has for us. If we accept Him as Lord and Savior, we need to learn to intentionally live like He taught us to. Accepting Him as savior is the intellectual acceptance of the mind. Accepting Him as Lord is the emotional acceptance of the heart. It takes both to live the lifestyle.

God longs to be in community with us, but he created us with free will, and He will never force Himself on us. We must freely choose Him, and He will reach out and touch us divinely with the indwelling of His Holy Spirit. Jesus said, "When He, the Spirit of Truth, has come, He will guide you in all truth; for He will not speak on His own authority, but whatever He hears He will speak; and He will tell you things to come." This is how we regain the purpose for which we were created, this is the way we fill the void sin had caused.

The Bible has numerous examples of God speaking directly to or through people, but I always thought that after He imparted His Holy Spirit to us that He spoke through him then, like to our conscience. Back in December 1984, my wife was eight and a half months pregnant with our third child when, one Friday, she couldn't feel the baby moving anymore. We went to the doctor, and an ultrasound revealed that the baby had turned in the womb and strangled itself on the umbilical cord. After a nightmarish weekend, we went in to try and induce labor to see if we could naturally abort her. Things moved swiftly; and soon, I was holding the beautiful body of my dead baby daughter. They sedated my wife, and she was soon asleep—much needed with all she'd been through—and I made my way down the hall to an empty waiting room.

I remember sitting there crying and praying, calling out to God, asking how he could let this happen, when a voice, as clear as if were right next to me, said, "You lost a child you never knew. I lost my son whom I knew forever." I opened my eyes and looked around, certain someone was right there, but I was alone. Yet, I wasn't alone, for the Father was right there with me, two fathers grieving the losses of their children. In perhaps the lowest point of my life, I received the greatest spiritual blessing, for God is always willing to meet His children at wherever we might be. As a post script to this story, the doctor recommended that though the baby looked normal and healthy, we should have an autopsy done. We consented and learned that the baby had a defective heart and would have required several surgeries at a minimum, and chances of survival were less than fifty percent. As a father, I would have mortgaged everything to try and save my baby, and it still may not have been enough. Did God allow this to happen because it saved us from financial ruin and may have ended in greater heartache by losing her later? I don't know. I can only be certain that He was with me every step of the way. And, eighteen months later, we were blessed with another baby girl—my beautiful Alisha Nichole. I am indeed blessed by my three children.

Religion is flawed because we are flawed, but Christianity is perfected through God's love for us. Many call themselves Christian today, yet I wonder how many do because it's expedient or politically correct, for they treat Christianity like a religion and not a way of life. Being a Christian in name only is not the same as being a Christ follower. I have learned that to be a Christ-follower means more than attending church on Sunday or following a set of rules. It means that I'm in a relationship with Him, that He is with me always. We talk and we share life together. He protects me and guides me, and I know I am a treasured child of the Most High God. It is intentionally living my faith. This is the most important aspect of wealthy living, for doing it right secures our eternal life after ours days on this earth are over. Everyone will experience eternal life after death—the question is, Where will you spend it?

Keep Loving!

What is love really? How do we define love? Is it even definitive? Can we put a relationship "to test" to see if it exemplifies "love?"

There are three types of love that I see in our society. First, there's the "I love you if…" style where love is conditional on specific action happening. "If you do (whatever) then I love you." Then there's the "I love you because…" style, again conditional on action, but usually already done. "Because you did (whatever) I love you." Last, there's the "I love you in spite of…" style, the unconditional love that says no matter what you do, I will love you. This is that "agape" love that Jesus Christ exemplified and taught. So, how can we determine if this is the type of love we practice, or do we "conditionalize" our love? Put your love to this test:

1. Do you find yourself getting impatient with your partner?
2. When you argue, do you bring up your partner's past faults or failings? Do you argue "the past?"
3. Are you selfish, or do you put your partner before you?
4. Do you get angry easily with your partner?
5. Are you envious?
6. Do you remain gracious, even in a dispute, or do you get rude?
7. Do you "remind" your partner how good you are?
8. Are you kind to your partner?
9. Do you protect your partner whenever possible?
10. Do you trust your partner?

11. Is the truth important to your relationship, or is honesty not a big issue?
12. Will your relationship persevere through trials?

We find perhaps the best definition of love in 1 Corinthians 13:4-7, it says, "Love is patient, love is kind. It does not envy, it does not boast, it is not proud. It is not rude, it is not self-seeking, it is not easily angered, it keeps no record of wrongs. Love does not delight in evil but rejoices with the truth. It always protects, always trusts, always hopes, and always perseveres." If we can examine ourselves and our relationship, and model this definition of love, how incredible our relationship would be.

Unfortunately, too many relationships sadly fail because the "love" is self-seeking and selfish. In our "instant gratification" society, our fast-food lifestyle, we've come to expect instant chemistry, instant "love," and aren't willing to invest the time and effort to grow something solid, something special. Infatuation is instant, and just as quickly, the bloom can fade; but love, true love takes time and withstands the tests of time. Time and commitment; it is the exact opposite of what society demands. No wonder divorce is such an attractive option today.

Love is misunderstood. Some think it's emotional. Some think it's a chemical reaction in our brain. Some think it's an evolutionary response to the opposite sex. But love is none of those things.

Certainly, there is an emotion that is associated with love. But it isn't love. It is necessary, however, in the whole process of love. That emotion, sometimes called "puppy love," is infatuation. More on that in a moment: But first, we need to examine love.

Pure and simple, love is choice. We don't fall in love; we choose to love. Love takes time, and it takes commitment. There is no "love at first sight," no instant soul mates. No, love takes time, that's why we need infatuation. There is "infatuation at first sight." Infatuation is that heart-fluttering, weak-in-the-knees feeling we get when we're strongly attracted to someone. When we first start to date someone, we can't wait to see them, we long to be with them when we're apart. We don't think we can live without them. We experience puppy love.

But that isn't love. That infatuation is what keeps bringing us back, time and again, as we get to know our heartthrob. We learn more about them through time, and, as that infatuation fades in time, we commit to our partner that we've gotten to know, just as they've grown to know us. Through time, we commit. We choose to love.

Sometimes, people mix up that feeling of infatuation with love; and when it fades, they move on, looking for someone to ignite that fire again and again, and in the end, they miss out on love altogether. Their life ends up being a string of shallow, ultimately meaningless relationships that left them empty and wanting. I had a Chinese instructor in college, teaching a "Marriage and the Family" class, as I pursued my degree in Human Relations. I'll never forget his teaching on love. He said infatuation usually lasts eighteen month to two years in a marriage, and then it begins to fade. Hopefully, in that time, true love has begun to grow, and it can carry the relationship forward. He then made a very interesting observation.

He said, "Love is not jealous. Infatuation is jealous." Being a young married student with my beautiful young wife working as the secretary for the college athletic director, with jocks and athletes constantly hanging around her, I had a little issue with that. I believed I was in "true love," but I was also sometimes bothered by the guys always hanging around my wife. So I asked him, wouldn't he be bothered if I hit on his wife? He responded no, and offered me cab fare to go try. After the class, I went up to him and told him I couldn't believe he wouldn't take issue with me trying to pick up his wife, and he explained it simply and beautifully. He had no problem with anyone trying to pick up his wife because he knew what her response would be. Her response would be appropriate. He then said he would only be bothered if his wife responded inappropriately. True love, over time, with commitment, doesn't have to worry about jealousy, for it knows the response will be appropriate.

Another aspect of love is that it is messy. Infatuation is neat, clean, well-mannered, and on its best behavior. When you begin dating someone, especially that first date or two, it's wise to look at that person across from you and remember, this is as good as it'll probably ever get. You see, on those first dates, each person is usually trying to impress, so they put their best foot forward. You see them on their best behavior, not their worst. Love is just the opposite. The more you love, the more open and vulnerable you become. You begin to show your partner all your warts and flaws; and as they are accepted, you open up and reveal more. True love is messy.

The best definition of love can be found in 1 Corinthians 13. It lays out what love is and isn't. This is an amazing definition of love. I can honestly say my love has fallen short of this definition more than once. But this is God's love, and it is perfect in itself because God is Love. That is what is most important to remember. In 1 John, John wrote, "God is love. Whoever lives in love lives in God, and God in him. In this way love is made complete among us so that we will have confidence on the Day of Judgment, because in this world we are like Him... We love, because He first loved us."

A couple of points about infatuation: first, it isn't a bad thing at all. It is the emotional stimulant that sometimes keeps a relationship exciting. It is that "falling in love" feeling. But it passes, and that's important to remember, for it will go away at some point. The biggest group of failed marriages is those of two years or less. The reason—infatuation fades and true love hasn't taken hold yet. Interestingly, the second largest group of failed marriages is "empty nesters." The kids grow up and move away; and suddenly, the two parents find that they've drifted apart and don't really know each other anymore. So, they split up and move on separately. That's sad because my second point about infatuation is this: it is entirely possibly to "fall in love" many times with the same person. As the emotions ebb, so they can flow. Sometimes, it just takes a little work to rekindle those "feelings." But loving someone isn't the same as falling in love. Love is time and commitment; falling in love is emotion.

There is another aspect to love that we often restrict. Love is vulnerable; and to truly love, you must prepare to make your heart vulnerable to the possibility of being hurt because if love goes wrong, our heart gets broken. All too often, after experiencing the pain of failed or unrequited love, we tend to wall off our heart to protect it from future pain. Yet, in doing, so we also restrict the possibility of fully loving again or even loving at all. Paul Simon wrote a song about this very thing. Some of the lyrics go:

> I am a rock. I am an island.
> I've built walls. A fortress deep and mighty
> That none may penetrate.
> I have no need of friendship; friendship causes pain
> Its laughter and its loving I distain.
> I am a rock. I am an island.
> Don't talk of love, but I've heard the words before.
> It's sleeping in my memory.
> I won't disturb the slumber of feelings that have died.
> If I never loved I never would have cried.
> I am a rock. I am an island.

This was a huge hit for Paul Simon, and I can't help but wonder if it touched a chord with those who loved and lost. It is sad to think of people choosing to withdraw instead of love. It truly is better to love and lose than to never love at all. And if you lose but are willing to put yourself back out there, to face the prospect of being vulnerable to the hurt again, you may just find that love your heart desires. But it only happens for those willing to be vulnerable.

Uniquely Unequal Love

I read somewhere that we do not love others equally; and as a father, my first thought was of my children and how I love them all the same. Yet, deeper introspection made me realize that I do not love all my children the same. I can honestly say that I love each with all my heart—in that they are equal, but that's where it ends. I came to realize that each child has impacted me differently; and with each one, I have a unique relationship and that causes me to love them uniquely different from each other. I don't love one necessarily "better" than another, just differently.

After I was able to come to terms with this epiphany, I began to do a little reminiscing about past relationships, both within my family and those of a romantic nature. I came to realize that not only do I love those I care or have cared about differently, that love has also changed through the course of the relationship and time. I also came to realize, especially in those of a romantic nature, that sometimes the ability to love was held captive by the past. I found that, especially in one instance, my partner was convinced that she's met "the love of her life." The relationship failed, and there would never be another. She had a long term relationship after her marriage that also failed, and she wasn't going to put herself out there and be hurt again.

I realize now that her desire was to experience that "first love" sensation that she once had, and you just can't duplicate love or the experience of love. That's why her second relationship failed. And the ensuing pain didn't allow her to try again, and our relationship failed. Each love relationship is unique, and to try to get it to conform to past ideals dooms it to failure. Let it live, grow, and experience the new and unique relationship—it's unique to you and your mate and no one else. It is yours to share together.

One lady I was with asked me about my past and was surprised to hear me say that I still love my ex-wife. And I still do and always will. And I love each woman God has brought into my life still, to this day, even though I have been terribly hurt by some—been lied to, deceived, robbed, rejected—it doesn't matter about the bad stuff in the end. Those are just the things that assure me we weren't made to be together forever. But each one loved me uniquely, for a time, as I did them, and those memories allow me to remember why I loved them and allow me to continue to love them for who they were to me. Memories are subjective, and we can choose to hang on to the good ones and remember why we loved. And that makes each and every relationship worthy no matter how it ended. Perhaps, one day, I will meet my "forever lady;" and when I do, I will love her completely and uniquely because those who were before helped teach me to love.

So a word to the wise: if it looks all neat and happens quickly, it might not be the real thing. If it's messy and has been percolating for some time, if you feel real committed to it, it might just be love!

Lighthouse Evangelism

I want to share a story here that impacted my life far greater than I ever imagined it would in the moment it happened. First, though, let me give some background. I was raised in a Christian household, a family of strong faith, which spread throughout my extended family. But, in our household, from my earliest recollections, it was my mother who was our spiritual rock, our hub that we radiated out from. My dad was very silent in his testimony, although he served faithfully on different church boards, always tithed, and for the most part seemed to do the right things.

I never wondered about my mother's faith for she taught us from her faith, but sometimes, I wondered about Dad because he never really talked about his faith, so I didn't know where he actually stood. Then, one day, I was at my dad's office at his car lot and my uncle, Dad's brother, was there. Now, my uncle, Brad, was very evangelical and very outspoken in his faith. He and his wife and kids would sing, play instruments, and share their testimonies at old folks' homes, apple orchards, and Salvation army—just about anywhere they could. This particular day, he was prodding my dad to come out to an event they were doing that weekend telling him he needed to be more involved, more outspoken. Dad declined, Brad pushed, Dad declined, and Brad pushed. Finally, Brad got up and told Dad he hoped he'd change his mind and he left.

I sat there a minute then said, "Dad, why don't you ever talk about your faith?"

Dad looked at me for a few seconds then said, "Bud, have you ever heard a lighthouse speak?"

I replied, "No, I haven't."

Dad said, "A lighthouse never says a word, but everyone knows what its message is."

At the time, it was a good answer, and it explained to me Dad's silence, but its impact wasn't fully felt until years later. In 2004, my dad had a horrific accident, breaking over thirty bones in his body, slipping into a coma for eleven days, and a very dark prognosis for any hope of recovery. It was one of the darkest periods of my life; but as it unfolded, I watched as we were contacted by person after person, praying for Dad, wishing us well. In all, I believe we heard from thirty-two states and people in several foreign countries. Cards, letters, prayer quilts, and calls all flooded in, and I was amazed at the number of lives my dad had touched who were reaching back to him. I remember recalling that incident with my uncle again and finally understanding how one can live a message, and it can be potent and powerful even without words. Dad miraculously recovered, and his doctors said it defied explanation. Well, yes and no—it defies explanation to those who don't know the healing power of Jesus.

Today, I've enjoyed thirteen years with my dad that the doctors never gave him, and I'm grateful for every time we're together, for every conversation by phone. I've learned to live like a lighthouse. Thank you, Dad.

Money

Money. Is it an end? Is it merely a means to an end? Is its accumulation a worthy goal or an empty dream? The pursuit of money, the lack of money, and the desire for money is at the root of more troubles, more evil than perhaps anything else. Money gives power, or so it is thought. Money buys things and things make us happy or so it is thought. The reality is money is none of these things. Money is nothing more than a tool.

I was raised in the church to believe that money was evil, and that those who had it were worldlier than those who didn't. That seemed to be the "religious" view of money. But that isn't the biblical view. Paul wrote to Timothy, "For the *love of money* is the root of all kinds of evil, for which some have strayed from the faith in their greediness, and pierced themselves through with many sorrow" (1 Tim. 6:10). Paul recognized that money is just a tool in life, but issues come into our lives when we lust after that tool. The love of money, not money itself, is the root of "all kinds" of evil—greed, cheating, and stealing—all kinds of wrongdoing stem from the love of money. In the end, money comes and money goes, but it's our attitude toward it that determines whether we've learned anything or not.

As a Christian, my faith is not in what money can or can't do for me, rather it is placing my faith in my God to meet all my needs. Paul writes, "And my God shall supply all your need according to His riches in glory by Christ Jesus" (Phil. 4:19). Now, I've heard people complain that "needs" aren't "wants," and what about things they want? God doesn't promise that, yet as I read Jesus's own words, in

John 14:13, he says, "And whatever you ask in My name that I will do, that the Father may be glorified in the Son. If you ask anything in My name I will do it." To me, that's pretty clear cut.

It should be noted, however, that this isn't a blank check to ask for all kinds of goodies. Jesus told His disciples that He is the vine and they the branches; and apart from Him, they can do nothing. In John 15:7, He says, "If you abide in Me, and My words abide in you, you shall ask what you desire and it shall be done for you. By this my Father is glorified, that you bear much fruit: so you will be my disciples." The key here is that we need to abide in Jesus, to live intentionally for Him; and if we do, then the desires of our heart will be in line with what He desires for us. There was a time, early in my marriage, when we struggled with only one vehicle. My oldest son was in school, my second one starting kindergarten, and mom and daughter still at home. I worked full-time, and it was a burden having just one vehicle, but we couldn't afford to buy a second car. I remember praying that asking for a car seemed like a lot, but He knew our needs. One evening, several nights later, I got a call from a missionary who was going back to the mission field, and he asked if I knew someone who could take his old car and use it. It had lots of miles, but it was a good car. I couldn't believe that God provided a car! I thanked him and shared my prayer. But that's the way God works. He always takes the route that gives Him the greatest glory.

There's another aspect of that passage that bears mentioning here, and it's Jesus's words that we should "ask whatever you will in My name, and I will do it." In this is My Father glorified, that you bear much fruit, proving to be My disciples. Now, I've heard preaching that said Jesus meant bearing much fruit glorifies the Father, and I've heard it preached that its proving to be His disciples that glorifies God. While I agree that both these things can bring glory to the Father, I don't think that was what Jesus meant. He said, "In this is my Father glorified," and what was He talking about? Asking "whatever you will in My name." Asking for things in Jesus's name brings glory to the Father!

The lesson then is not to get hung up on money, or the things it can buy, but trust God to supply our wants and needs. He is more than capable of meeting all our needs according to His purpose. And life is so much easier allowing Him to carry the money burden. Through my years as a small business owner, many times arose when cash flow was short, or I needed extra for something. I prayed for God to help in those times, and never once did He let me down when I waited on Him! (And now, my son, Ryan, is experiencing similar answers to prayer as he owns the business!)

The leading conflict in marriages is monetary issues. Can you imagine if more couples could learn to trust God about money, how much stronger marriage could be? Instead of fussing and fretting, couples could be claiming His promises and rejoicing together! It's all about faith. It's all about allowing God to work in His time, for His timing is never wrong. God always takes the route that brings Him the greatest glory.

With all that being said, here are some practical pointers when it comes to your money and what you do with it. First, you need to honor God with it (see Tithing). Next, pay your obligations—bills, mortgage, food, etc. What is left is often where we run into trouble, and in two specific areas—investing and loans. First, investing; many people want to invest in the stock market, but just don't know how. This subject could be a whole book in itself. But, for now, let me say don't invest any money that you can't afford to lose. The market has created far more paupers than princes. But if you decide to invest, you should research how to invest yourself, and start small with an account you manage yourself, such as Think or Swim, Ameritrade, or E-trade to name a few. There, you pay between five and ten dollars per trade, rather than forty to sixty to a broker. Next, remember this, the trend is your friend! Follow the trend of what the market is doing, and invest accordingly. You rarely make money bucking the trend of the market. And last, don't fall in love with your investments. If you own a stock and it rises significantly, sell it or at least sell off enough to recoup your investment. You can let the profits ride if you want, for that's "free money" in the market. Protect you investment!

When it comes to loans, and here I'm talking about you making a loan to someone, remember these points. When you lend, be prepared never to get it back. Just have that frame of mind because when you're approached for money, it's usually a friend or loved one; and if they need your money, it's often because they can't get it anywhere else. The odds are pretty fair you may not get your money back for a long time, if ever. Still, you can protect yourself by putting everything in writing. And make sure you put everything in writing because down the road, it will become your word against theirs, and feelings will be hurt. I learned this the hard way. I used to keep some money on hand for emergencies and on occasion loaned some out to family or friends. I was in a Bible study once and had help out a member or two with loans that were paid back per agreement. One night, after the study, a newer member approached me and said they had a need, and one of our leaders recommended they talk to me. She said she and her husband needed five hundred dollars and couldn't raise the money. I agreed to help, so she said she would bring her husband back tomorrow.

The next day, the couple showed up, and we sat down to talk about it. Only overnight their need grew—now they needed fifteen hundred. It seemed that he was a fledgling comedian and need the money to finish a CD and start his career in comedy. He was a local radio celebrity, so I thought they'd be a safe risk. They asked what kind of interest rate I wanted, and I told them no interest—just pay back the principal when they can. It was very casual and open-ended. Well, a year passed, and I received nothing from this couple; but on his radio show, the guy was talking about all this expensive workout equipment they'd bought that now was covered with clothes, etc., so I decided to call and see what was going on.

The wife answered; and when I asked when I could expect some payments on their loan, she actually got indignant and told me I didn't loan them money—it was a gift. I assured her it was a loan, but because I refused any interest, she assumed I wasn't interested in any payback. I asked her to have her husband call me. When he did, he acknowledged the loan and agreed to begin making payments; and in time, they paid it off. However, the wife was very begrudging, and it ended up ruining a friendship, though casual as it was. Since then, I put everything in writing, and just say it's for both of our benefits, so we both understand the terms of our loan. That way, if there is an issue, it's not your issue.

Now: The Time to Live

We are a goal-oriented society, driven by our goals and dreams. From graduating high school and on to college, graduating college and entering the work place, to become that which we dreamed of becoming through all our years of toil and study, we strive to accumulate wealth, prestige, and honors so that our golden years will be happy years, but they won't.

For you see, life doesn't happen when we achieve our goals. Our happiness is not found in the culmination of our dreams. Meeting goals leads to a sense of emptiness. So where is happiness found? Where is life the grandest? It is here, and now, as we struggle to achieve, as we push ever forward in hopes of achieving. Life and happiness is happening now. It is our job to recognize it and embrace it. I've heard people say things like, "Where have the years gone?" or, "I never really knew my kids," all because they were so caught up in the dream that they missed life as it happened all around them. Life is now. Happiness is found in recognizing life and embracing the good as it happens. A baby's first word or step, a delicious meal prepared by your mate, a humming bird feeding outside your window, or a gentle caress—there are a multitude of things happening all around us each and every day that can bring a smile to our lips or put a song in our heart. We need to be aware, to live in the moment, to embrace that life happening around us to really find happiness. Life and happiness are not in the meeting of our goal or our dreams; it is in the struggle, the journey, and the path to get there.

Life is lived only in one place—the present. Unfortunately, all too often, we find ourselves distracted from life, even as it's happening to us, by the past or the future. I remember so clearly as a boy that "time" just seemed to drag by. Years were measured by halves and quarters ("I'm seven and a half," or "I'm eleven and three quarters"). I couldn't wait for each milestone to come. I lived often for the future, and it seemed to take forever to arrive.

As I get older, I'm amazed at how fast time passes and often wonder what happened to my summer or lament on things I didn't get done that I wanted to accomplish wondering where the time went. All too often, I'm distracted by my past. I tell myself I'm going to do things as I look to the future, yet often forgetting that one unchangeable truth—life is happening now. Sometimes, I find myself talking to someone, or doing some task, and my mind is on a dozen other things, other places, distracted by was or is to come.

Life is happening now, all around us, and it is in our best interest to learn to live in the moment, to be aware of now, and all that is happening around us. This is life, and this is where our joy and contentment lie. The past is gone, the future may never come, but we have today. We need to learn to own it. By owning each day, by doing what we can right now, in the present, to make our lives better, is the secret to a better tomorrow. No one owes you anything more than you have today. Take advantage of what you have while you have it, and refocus yourself on now.

Living in awareness of life, embracing each day, each moment, and finding our moments of happiness there fills our lives with memories. In my relationships, I've had both positive and negative memories occur, which is normal. But as I've earlier shared, I've learned to take those negative memories and couch them between two positive ones—something good that happened prior and something good that happened afterwards—and I've found that the bitterness of the negative memory, and often the memory itself, fades away; and I'm left with pleasant memories of days gone by. And that's where our happiness in our Golden years is found, in the memories of all that was good in our journey. So, don't miss out on life today hoping that it'll be grander tomorrow, for it won't, and you will have robbed yourself another day and potentially many moments of future memories. Seize the day; live in the moment; and stop and smell the roses, you'll be glad on day that you did.

The Opposite of Love

I remember building a fire not so long ago. As it burned, I noticed how all-consuming fire is. I also noticed it burned differently depending on the wood. I had a couple of pieces of oak, solid, heavy wood that was still burning when I came in at midnight. Several pieces of Aspen burned quick and bright, but didn't last long at all. I had some pine that flared up nice, but also burned quickly.

I got to thinking that fire is a lot like some of our emotions. Those emotions that are powerful and strong are like fire. Love is fire. It can start out slow, small, and not real hot; but in time, it grows, in size, in heat, and in intensity. Like different kinds of wood, we can also experience love differently from a stable long-burning emotion to the white-hot flare up that recedes and leaves us sometimes confused and spent.

But love is not alone in being an intense emotion. Hate is also a fire. Often, hate is thought to be the opposite of love, but it is not. It is perhaps better described as love's cousin, for it is very similar to love in its characteristics. It can start slow and build. It can become intense and all-consuming relationally because they are so similar in their intensity. People often fluctuate between these powerful emotions within the relationship. Factor in the powerful emotion of anger as the catalyst between the two, and it's easy to understand the concept of a love-hate relationship. There is a very fine line between the two because they can be so intense and consuming.

So what is the opposite of love? The opposite of love is indifference. Like a fire, love needs to be fed and to be fueled if it is going to grow in heat and intensity. Failure to feed the fire allows the fire to die, and the fault is ours; for like fire, it needs our attention to survive and to grow. Indifference is like wet wood—there's no way fire will ever be able to consume it, for it is incapable of allowing even the smallest spark to take hold. Indifference is the antithesis of love; it is the killer of relationships. Beware of indifference!

Parents

One thing that we all share in common is that we have parents. Some, though, may never have had the chance to know their parents, while others spend a lifetime getting to know theirs. But being a parent is far more than being on one end of a biological hook-up that happens to fertilize an egg and create a pregnancy. No, being a parent means investing your time, energies, and yourself into your child. Some of the best parents in the world are adoptive parents because they chose to be parents, they were intentional in their desire. As parents, we have the responsibility for raising our children, for teaching them right from wrong, teaching them social graces, and teaching them how to deal with what life throws at you. Parenting can be overwhelming at first.

I've always maintained that our structure is backwards. It seems that just about the time we figure the whole parenting thing out, our kids are grown and out on their own. We have all this valuable information and no one to share it with because our kids already know everything, and part of the joy of moving out on their own was they did not have to listen to parents anymore. Then they start having kids; and suddenly, our information is valuable. But now, we're learning a whole new set of skills—grand parenting! Now, we learn how to spoil our grandkids, which is entirely opposite of good parenting, causing our children to ask, "Who are these people? I didn't grow up with them." I say, sugar up the grand kids and send them home! I remember visiting my oldest son after he had his first child, my granddaughter. We had run to the grocery store for a few items; and during the trip, he said to me, "Dad, I don't know how you did it. You had three kids at my age, all under ten years old. We're going to have our second, and I can't handle another one." I remember assuring him that he'd do fine, that he'd figure it out like all young parents have to do, and to his credit, he's done wonderfully. But there for a moment, it was nice being appreciated.

As I've acquired grandkids, I have received confirmation from all my kids that they better appreciate me as a father as they learn to parent. To their credit, they are all wonderful parents. They are also wonderful children as adults. They have embraced adulthood and accepted the responsibilities that come with it despite obstacles that may get in their way. Today, too many adult millennials are falling back on the safety net of their parents, returning to their parents' home as adults because they find difficulty making it on their own. Usually, it is a combination of school debt, credit card debt, and poor credit ratings that drive them back because they haven't learned intentional living or how to curb their need for instant gratification. Suddenly, in a time the parents should be at the stage where they can enjoy life and face retirement, many are forced to continue working to support grown kids who returned to the nest unexpectedly. As parents, we love our children and want to help them; but in taking them back in, we are really doing them a disservice, for we are enabling them instead of allowing them to figure it out on their own.

Another aspect of parenting is the whole aging process. I've given great thought to how I want my children to deal with me when that time comes that I can't live alone. I really hate the idea of an old folk's home, so I propose the following:

Rather than go into a home, I just book continuous cruises on these major cruise ships. A current survey of nursing home costs puts it at $70,080 per year or about $192 per day. Conversely, I can do a six-day cruise for $250-300 or $50 per day. For sake of argument, let's say the cost of a cruise doubles over the next few years while nursing home care remains fiscally constant. Let's look at what I get for *half* the money.

I can have *ten* meals a day if I can only waddle to the restaurant or buffet, or I can have room service (breakfast in bed every day!).

I have workout rooms, steam rooms, swimming pools, hot tubs, spas, washers and dryers, Vegas-quality shows every night, a casino, plus much, much more.

I get free toothpaste, razors, soap, and shampoo.

My towels and sheets are changed daily, and I don't even have to ask!

If there's a light bulb out, or the TV goes on the fritz, or if I want a different mattress, no problem—they fix it right away and apologize for the inconvenience.

I get to meet new people every seven to fourteen days.

I'm treated like a customer, not a patient. Staff scrambles to help.

And best of all, I'd get to see South America, the Caribbean, Australia, New Zealand, Europe, Tahiti, Mexico, or wherever I might want to go!

I'm thinking there's not going to be a nursing home in my future. Look for an old guy hanging at the rail taking in the glorious sunsets. I can't think of a drawback to this plan. If I fall and break a hip in a home, I go on Medicare; if I fall and break a hip on a cruise ship, I get upgraded to a suite—probably for life!. So I think I'll cruise 'til I die—then it's a burial at sea—no charge!

Quality Humor

A huge part of life has to be humor. I read a statistic once that said the average baby smiles an average of four hundred times a day. Conversely, an adult smiles an average of only fifteen times a day. Somewhere, through the course of growing up, we lost 385 smiles a day. It is far easier to smile than to frown, and there's something therapeutic about laughter. With that said, I thought we should dedicate some space to things that may bring us a smile. The following are quips, questions, and quotes to loosen the laughter:

Did Adam have a belly button?

If I travel at the speed of light and turn on my headlights, what happens?

It is said that if one is capable of traveling faster than the speed of light, then he would actually travel backwards in time. If I could travel fast enough, could I get to where I am going before I actually leave?

Why are they called paper clips if they're metal?

If I were to ship a load of Styrofoam, what should I pack it in?

Why do we call it a "hot water heater?" If the water's hot, why heat it? If it's cold, then we should call it a "cold water heater."

Why do we drive on parkways and park on driveways?

Why do we call a delivery by truck a "shipment," but a delivery by ship "cargo"?

What was the greatest thing before sliced bread?

When two planes almost collide, it's called a "near miss." Wouldn't a near miss be a hit?

If 7-11 stores advertise they're open 24 hours a day, 365 days a year, then why do they have locks on their doors?

If the little black box is so indestructible, why don't they make the whole plane out of it?

If you choke a Smurf, what color does it turn?

If nothing sticks to Teflon, then how does it stay on the pan?

If you make a cow laugh real hard, would milk come out its nose?

Why don't we spell Phonetic the way it sounds?

Why are there interstate highways in Hawaii?

Before drawing boards were invented, what did we go back to?

What hair color do they put on a bald man's driver's license?

If a book about failures doesn't sell, is it a success?

Do cemetery workers prefer the graveyard shift?

And some favorite signs I've seen:
NO SOLICITING
We are too broke to buy anything.
We already know who we're voting for.
WE HAVE FOUND JESUS.
Seriously. Unless you are selling thin mints
PLEASE GO AWAY!

"Wine is better with age. I am better with wine."

"If I turn up missing, I want my picture put on wine bottles instead of milk cartons. That way, my friends will know to look for me."

And to my siblings, "We are different flowers from the same garden."

And, "I smile because you are my sister. I laugh because you can do nothing about it!"

"I'm so busy I don't know if I found a rope or lost my horse!"

"Marriage is like a deck of cards. In the beginning, you need two hearts and a diamond. By the end, you wish you had a club and a spade."

And, finally, my two favorites:
"Sweat is fat crying."
"Sometimes, I laugh so hard tears run down my leg!"

As I am now a grandfather, soon to be six times over, I thought I should collect a few children's books for when I have visits from the grandkids. Sure, I could get Bambi, Snow White, Jungle Book, and the other regular Disney stuff, but I wanted to be different; so I've scoured the used book stalls for those unique or different ones. I'm thinking perhaps these titles are not the best for the grand-kids:

The Boy Who Died From Eating All His Vegetables
Fun 4-Letter Words to Know and Share
A Toddler's Guide to Hitchhiking
Dad's New Wife Robert
The Popup Book of Human Anatomy
Why Can't Mr. Fork and Mrs. Electrical Outlet Be Friends?
Pop Goes the Hamster—And Other Fun Microwave Games
Strangers Have the Best Candy
Your Nightmares Are Real
And, Daddy Drinks Because You Cry...
(Perhaps those tried and true Disney stories are best after all).

I would be remiss if I didn't include a couple old favorite jokes:
There was an old couple, married so sixty-five years, and now the wife is ailing and on her death bed. She calls her husband over and says, "Honey, we've had a good marriage, and we've always been honest with each other—no secrets, except for that shoebox I keep in the closet that I asked you never to open. It's time you open it."

He went to the closet and, with trembling hands, brought the box to her bedside. She reached down and pulled the ribbon that tied it shut. He lifted the lid, and there inside were two crocheted dolls and ninety-three thousand dollars!

She said to him, "Honey, when we got married, my old grandma took me aside and said, 'Any time you get angry with him, just crochet a doll. By the time you're done, your anger will have passed.'"

His old eyes misted over, seeing just two dolls in the box after sixty-five years.

"But where did all the money come from?" he asked.

"Oh, that's what I made from selling dolls!"

Charlie had a drinking problem; and, finally, his wife had enough. She told him the next time he came home drunk that was it, he was out! Well, Charlie did real well for a couple weeks, but then one night, while out bowling with his buddies, he tied one on. He came home drunk; and while trying to quietly sneak up the stairs, he slipped and fell. In the tumble, he broke a bottle of gin in his back pocket, cutting up his derriere pretty good. He went in the bathroom, cleaned it all off, and bandaged himself up. He then went back upstairs and slipped into bed, never waking his wife. The next morning, she came in. "Charlie, you came home drunk last night, didn't you? You came home drunk and had an accident, right?"

"What? How did you know?"

"Why, there are Band-Aids all over the mirror!"

And finally,

The Lone Ranger and Tonto had been out chasing bandits all day; and finally, at sundown, rode into town. They pulled up in front of the saloon, and the Lone Ranger indicated he wanted to go in for a beer. Tonto told him he would cool off the horses first, got an Indian blanket, and began running around the horses, fanning them.

The Lone Ranger had just ordered his beer and sat down at the bar when a cowboy came in.

"Who owns that big white horse out front?" he asked.

"I do," said the Lone Ranger. "Why?"

"Well, you left your engine (injun) running."

(As I have Native American blood in me, I feel I can tell this joke without worrying about political correctness).

Relationships

I was describing myself, sort of tongue-in-cheek, to someone, and said, "I'm a simple man, yet complex in my simplicity. I am an enigma wrapped in a conundrum. That's me in a nutshell."

The response was, "What kind of nutshell?"

After a moment's thought, I replied, "Walnut."

When pressed why walnut, I explained that walnut shells are somewhat unique in their rough exteriors but house a pretty good nut inside. They're a little rough and sometimes tough to crack, but what's inside is usually worth the effort.

That got me thinking about others, and how, in reality, we all wrap ourselves in one sort of shell or another. We all tend to protect our inner selves, to insulate ourselves from the potential hurt of others by hiding in or behind our emotional shells. Some call them walls; and the reality is, to really experience community with others, to meet that emotional void that only community can fill, we need to let others in, and we need to allow others to crack our shell and get to the meat of who we really are.

Unfortunately, in all too many cases, who we really are is not someone we ourselves like. And if we cannot like ourselves, much less love ourselves, how can we expect another person to like or love us? Self-worth, self-esteem is so important in creating an environment that fosters the trust that another can like and even love us for who and what we are. Until we can learn to love ourselves, we cannot truly love another, nor can we feel the confidence that they truly love us. Self-acceptance is the first step toward a truly loving relationship with another person. Self-acceptance is one of the prerequisites for any successful friendship or relationship.

The key to total acceptance, whether for self or others, is learning to dispense grace. To accept is to forgive, for we all do wrong, to ourselves, to others. Grace is unmerited forgiveness. God forgives us though we've done nothing to deserve it, and if we can truly accept this fact, then we can in turn forgive both our wrongs as well as the wrongs of others. Dispensing grace is as enriching for the dispenser as for the one dispensed, for in emulating one of God's attributes, we can come to more fully appreciate what He has done for us. Dispensing grace can be a completely humbling act.

Two cornerstones to successful relationships are honesty and trust. Trust is the glue, which allows people who are uniquely different to bond; and while that trust is pure and unbroken, it is so strong that the relationship can withstand virtually anything. However, once the trust bond is broken, we find out how fragile trust itself really is. It is not impossible to repair trust once it is violated, but it is a difficult process, and it takes time. Honesty is usually a casualty of broken trust, for when we break trust, we tend to lie to cover ourselves. Honesty and trust, along with our self-acceptance, are the cornerstones of strong, vital relationships. Infidelity is the biggest killer of honesty and trust, and easily the number one relationship killer.

There are other relationships killers though, for example, sex. Personally, I don't see any redeeming social value in it. Sex is a selfish act performed by selfish people who are afraid of relational depth and commitment, and usually have very little self-esteem. Pretty harsh words, but true. Sex is something you can get from a prostitute or an escort service, and it has one primary function: Meet my carnal needs.

Now, making love, on the other hand, is a beautiful expression of two people uniting as one with the primary focus to meet the needs and desires of one's mate. It is a culmination of getting to know someone, of exploring and learning about our mate, and of desiring to know one deeper more intimately. It is a result of learning to love someone, and its primary focus is on the other. Love making is self-less. It is far more than merely a physical act of gratification; it is a bonding physically, emotionally, and even spiritually.

So why do so many people seek/choose sex today? Why are there so many one night stands, bar hook ups, etc.? I think people are so desperate to connect, to find love, that they jump into bed before they even know the other person. How can you love someone if you don't even know if you like them? And sex has set the tone for any furtherance of a possible relationship. The initial focus is wrong; the possibility of success is not good, for the focus is "meet my needs."

If the initial focus, when meeting someone, is to get to know them, and as a relationship begins to develop, to put their wants and desires first, as they choose to put yours ahead of theirs, then a giving, nurturing relationship develops. It is just the opposite of sex, which says "satisfy me." A nurturing environment develops, and love can grow where nurtured. But love, true love, takes time. Time and commitment, and those two things will never be found in a one-night stand. So, if you really want to find love, then promise yourself that you'll invest the time needed to discover it and allow it to grow. Don't just respond to that physical urge, that lust, and that infatuation. Give yourself and your possible relationship the best odds of making it. Don't just have sex, hold out for making love—you'll never regret it!

Another thing that can be deadly to a relationship is emotional blackmail. This would include saying things like, "If you really loved me…" or, "Just back me on this if you really care for me…" or, "If you really valued our relationship…" or, "What are we gonna tell the kids?" or any other of a myriad of statements that shift the focus from the real issue to your relationship. When one tries to make the relationship more important than the issue at hand, that diversion is emotional blackmail.

The reality is the one who makes such statements is actually threatening you, and you need to protect yourself, at least mentally. And the first step to protecting yourself is to be clear as to what is happening. You need to ask yourself, "If I don't yield to this veiled threat, will they really harm our relationship?" Is my love/affection really being challenged, or is it a ploy to manipulate me into a desired action/reaction by my mate? You need to refocus the attention back onto the issue at hand, and take the relationship aspect off the table.

You might want to respond with something like, "My love/affection (etc.) has nothing to do with the issue at hand. The problem is…" Restating the issue can, and refusing to yield to blackmail will either make you stronger or possibly elicit a very negative reaction from your mate, even to the point that they sever the relationship. If something that extreme happens because you stand up to their emotional blackmail, the odds are strong that that was a very unhealthy relationship to start with and wouldn't have withstood the test of time. People who use this tactic are emotional bullies and usually prey upon those who are co-dependent or suffer from low self-esteem. Don't give in to emotional blackmail—it's never worth sacrificing your core values or beliefs just to appease your mate. The truth is, if they really loved you, they wouldn't stoop to such tactics.

Another killer of relationships is unabated anger. Anger is not wrong. Everyone gets angry at something or someone, sooner or later. It is an often misunderstood emotion, for it is not a bad in itself. Unbridled anger or uncontrolled anger is a bad thing and can destroy a relationship. When we allow our anger to run unbridled, we say things and do things that can't be undone. Yes, we can forgive anger, but we really don't forget the intentional hurtful things that are said or done out of anger. As my Grandma used to say, "Once a word is said, it's dead, some say. I say, it just begins to live that day."

Uncontrolled anger will drive a couple further apart and will make reconciliation that much more difficult. If our desire is to be together and to live in a harmonious relationship then uncontrolled anger is our enemy. The solution is anger management. Learn to control your temper, and you won't regret your words or actions even if you're angry. Sometimes, it means walking away for a while, to regain control. Sometimes, it means choosing not to respond to hurtful things said while emotions are running high. And yet, when one partner can't control their anger, their tongue, they are emotionally abusive, and no one deserves to be abused. The end of the relationship should be near when anger controls a person, for their right to express anger inappropriately ends where your nose begins.

Another relationship killer is lying. That *lying is wrong* is virtually a universally accepted tenant, and, yet, it is violated by virtually everyone. Little white lies, lies of omission, lies about our past, lies to cover actions, and lies to try to avoid trouble—no matter what the form, a lie is a lie. It is an untruth, and it erodes the very foundation of any relationship. For truth must be part of the foundation for any relationship to be successful.

So why do we lie? The first lie was told in the Garden of Eden when Satan first approached Eve and tempted her with the forbidden fruit. "You will be like God," he said, "if you only eat of the fruit. God forbid it because He didn't want you to be like Him." It was a crafty lie, and a crafty argument. After all, who wouldn't want to be like God? And that first lie destroyed a relationship between man and God. God later restored it, but it remains in a broken state as long as we live in a broken world.

Ever since that first lie, the art of lying has destroyed relationship after relationship because you can't trust a liar, for you can never be sure they're telling you the truth. And without the inability to trust, the relationship is dead or soon will be. Our world is full of lies—our courts, our politicians, our advertising, TV, and our workplaces. We are bombarded by lies all day long. Is it no wonder people find it easier to lie than to be truthful? Lies cover up; truth reveals.

The beauty of telling the truth, and this is a lesson so few have learned, is that you don't have to remember anything when you're honest. The truth is the truth—there's nothing to remember. And, yet, when we lie, we must remember the lie, for more often than not, we end up building on it. Lie upon lie, until one day, the house of lies we built comes crashing down when we stumble or get caught in one of our untruths. Lies cover up; truth reveals. To live an open and authentic life is one of the greatest and most rewarding challenges we face today, yet so few are willing to step up and meet that challenge. I will, and I hope you will too.

The last of the relationship killers is failure to communicate. Breakdowns in communication are often a major factor in the failure of relationships. The question isn't so much why communication breaks down, rather what are the reasons behind the lack of communication, for anyone can learn to communicate—it becomes a matter of the will to do so. Communication is not just learning to say how you feel or what you think, it is also learning to constructively listen to our mate and respond appropriately. Communication can be learned, but it isn't effective until desired.

People handle their emotions in different ways. Some wear their emotions on their sleeve and need to address issues immediately. They're usually the "exploders," who go off and then feel better. Then there's the "stuffers," who just take everything in and compact it, like a trash compactor, until it's too full and garbage can't help but leak out. And there's the "stealth bomber," who takes all the heat, then, usually on the way out, takes a shot back and disappears. None are healthy ways to deal with our emotions, and all lead to a failure to effectively communicate.

To effectively communicate, we need to get past the emotions of the situation and deal with the issue. Sometimes, that means just walking away for a time, to let emotions cool, and then attempting to address the issue when things are calmer. But it isn't healthy to just walk away without communicating anything, that could be misconstrued as you are walking out on the relationship/issue/person. It needs to be clearly stated that, for the good of our relationship, perhaps we need a couple hours to cool off, or a day, weekend, etc. Everyone cools off differently, but trying to address an emotion-charged issue is almost always a lose-lose proposition.

Anyone can learn to communicate effectively. It is a choice to learn to do so or else to continue to fail in this critical area. People who choose not to learn to listen and to share their feelings are usually demonstrating a passive aggression towards their mate and relationship, which will ultimately result in failure.

Back in 2006, I started a blog called "Thoughts-Outside-The-Box," and in September of 2007, wrote a short blog called "Inequitable Relationships." Since its publication it has been read or searched of roughly forty times more than my average post, and more than four times more than my next most popular post. Why are these statistics important? Because relationships are so important to living a successful and intentional life. If my little inconsequential blog gets that kind of traffic on the subject, then it shows a real interest in relationships, and further, a desire to be in good ones. The question begs to be asked, "If relationships are so critical to us then why can they be so difficult?"

To fully understand relationships, it is important to start at the beginning, the very first recorded relationship. God created Adam to be in community with Him. He created Eve as a companion to Adam, to share in that community. And ever since, we have an ingrained need for community, to be in relationships with others, and ultimately, with God. It is in community with God that we find completeness; it is in community with others we learn how to be in community with God. We are social beings. Yet, we run into problems with our relationships because we are flawed, imperfect. Just as Adam separated from God through his original disobedience, we find ourselves separated from perfect community, perfect relationship. We find that relationships take effort, they're work. And all too often, we reject relationships that require too much effort.

The Fifty-Fifty Relationship

One of biggest relational failures stem from the fifty-fifty relationship mind-set. When two people get together, they mentally begin to assess the work involved. They may even discuss the parameters of the relationship, agreeing to who will do what. Fifty-fifty; each does their half and the relationship is smooth sailing, right? Wrong. We will inevitably fail to uphold our end and, even if through some miracle we do, our partner will at some point fail. The result is discord, arguments, and disharmony. Too often, the offended party has to pick up the slack, to right the relationship. The dynamics of the relationship may begin to shift, perhaps to a sixty-forty or even a seven-thirty type of split. Resentment builds. Anger replaces that feeling of love. The couple distances from each other until, finally, they split, wondering what they ever saw in each other in the first place.

A solution is to change your mind-set. Sit down with your partner and agree to each give 100 percent, no matter what. Some days, you will fail in that, but your partner will be there to pick up the slack. And some days, they will fail, and you will pick up the slack. There's still no guarantee that your relationship will be successful, but a 100 percent understanding is a good building block for success.

Team Building

Another building block in any successful relationship is to determine, in a time of calm reflection, that both parties want to be in the relationship. If both "sides" determine and agree that their bottom line is that their desire is to be in the relationship, then the reality is you are both on the same side. There are no "sides" in an argument because the bottom line is you both share the same ultimate desire to be in that relationship. I was in a relationship once with a woman with a severe anger management problem. It seemed that every time we had a disagreement, she went right to "we're done!" and we split up. When she cooled down, be it hours, days, or weeks, she would want to reestablish the relationship. This went on for several years until I learned this principle. Then, when she would go to that "we're done!" place, I would remind her that my bottom line is to be with her and ask if hers was still to be with me. If she answered affirmatively, I then would ask, "What do I have to do to restore our relationship?" This question is key for two reasons.

First, the question doesn't demand that your partner change their behavior. It says that "I" am willing to do whatever it takes to restore things. Even if their anger is outrageous and out of control, it says to them "I" am making the effort. The second thing it does is it elicits a response from your partner as to what they want you to do to restore harmony. In doing so, they must revisit the cause of the disharmony to address it. Most often, they realize they have fault too and are more willing to address it knowing you are a willing partner. For the record, this worked wonders a number of times in my relationship until the time I was told that her bottom had changed—she didn't want to be with me anymore. With that response, I sadly left the relationship and didn't return despite her later "changes of heart." It takes two working together to make a successful relationship, but it only takes one to destroy it.

Inequitable Relationships

The most difficult of all relationships are those that are inequitable. Unfortunately, they are also the most common. It is rare indeed that two people get the exact same out of a relationship; and when they don't, it becomes inequitable for one of the parties. Relationships are like living things though; they can ebb and flow in their inequities between the parties and often do. Whether one is having a bad day, week, or trial of some kind, often, the relationship suffers because one's focus is on the trial at hand and not giving one's all to the relationship. It is then when the other partner needs to step up and carry the relational load until balance can be restored. There should be a give-and-take aspect to any successful relationship.

Problems occur when a relationship becomes inequitable and one partner abuses this state. The ebb and flow of the relationship stalls and the burden of the relationship falls to one party to carry it. Usually, the partner who becomes more invested in the relationship is the one that becomes abused. Most often, this investment is emotional, and that's the easiest to abuse. The one who is more invested tends to shoulder the load for their partner until it becomes burdensome and stressful. Then it seems the problems start, but the reality is they started some time ago and are now manifesting themselves because the invested partner has "had enough." It sometimes comes as a shock to the other partner because they've just been skating along, thinking all is rosy in their world. It becomes incumbent on them to step up and change, or the relationship is headed for serious trouble, for the emotionally invested partner is normally more vulnerable more open to hurt. If the offending partner doesn't respond to the relationship and restore it to its normal ebb and flow there will be serious consequences. Many relationships don't survive if the abusive partner refuses to change.

Christian Relationships

There has been much debate through the years about exactly what Paul meant when he addressed marriage in Ephesians 5:22–33. This is the passage that Paul says that wives should submit to their husbands, for he is the head of the family as Christ is the head of the church. A couple points need to be made here; first, the passage doesn't say husbands get your wives to submit. The submission is strictly the responsibility of the wife, and not the husband. She will be blessed by God for obeying or disciplined by Him if she doesn't. The second point is the translation of the word "submit." It is also used as a military term in reference to officers under a commander and literally means to get underneath and lift one up, or to support. That is a far cry from absolute obedience as some Christian men have petitioned for. As for those Christian men, they too are commanded to action, and their responsibility is to love their wives as Christ loved the church. Remember, Christ sacrificed everything for the church, including His own life that the church might grow and prosper. Do we love our wives that sacrificially? I dare say, a woman who has that kind of love poured out on her would have little problem submitting to her husband.

Relationships are work. I've heard people say that "it shouldn't be this hard" to make relationships work, but they're wrong. They are work because they are living and always evolving; and if we don't work at them, they'll evolve into the wrong direction. They take time and effort. Think of them like they're your lawn. If you feed, water, weed, and mow it, you end up with a beautiful showpiece that's the envy of the neighborhood. But if you let it go, only occasionally paying it attention, you end up with a ragged mess full of weeds and problems, and no one envies you. Things come and go, but your relationships can last a lifetime. Nurture them, help them blossom into beautiful things, and you will have beautiful memories when you are old.

Success through Failure

The best results in life revolve around failures—our failures. Sure, it's nice to succeed, but continual success doesn't lead to a rich and fulfilling life. That is only achieved through failure, or more specifically, dealing with failure in a proper mind-set.

Continued success robs us of appreciation and diminishes the value of our success. Failure, on the other hand, makes us all the more aware of the beauty of our accomplishments once we finally do succeed. And appreciation is a necessary ingredient to a rich and fulfilled life. Our greatest success stories are often founded on lives that experienced bitter failure. It wasn't the failure that is important to note, but that each time, our heroes picked themselves up, dusted them off, and tried again. And when they finally did succeed, their success was all the more rich and rewarding because of what they went through to obtain it. Here are just a few examples:

There was once a man who went to war with the rank of captain. He left the war with the rank of private. He then went into business, but his business failed. He studied law, but failed there too, criticized for being too impractical and temperamental. He turned to politics, but was defeated in his first attempt at the legislature, then was defeated in his first attempt at Congress, and was defeated in his bid to be commissioner of the General Land Office. He was then defeated in his senatorial bid, and next, defeated in attempt to win the vice-presidency, then defeated in a senatorial bid again. He wrote to a friend, "I am now the most miserable man living. If what I feel were equally distributed to the whole human family, there would not be one cheerful face on earth." Who was this man? Our 16th President, Abraham Lincoln.

Another popular hero, Michael Jordan, once commented, "I've missed more than nine thousand shots in my career. I've lost almost three hundred games. Twenty-six times, I've been trusted to take the game-winning shot and missed. I've failed over and over and over again in my life. That's why I succeed."

Thomas Edison failed a thousand times before inventing the incandescent light bulb. A reporter asked him how it felt to fail a thousand times and he replied, "I didn't fail one thousand times. The light bulb was an invention with a thousand steps." Confucius said, "Our greatest glory is not in never failing, but in rising every time we fall." Charles Kettering said, "Failing is one of the greatest arts in the world. One fails toward success."

Henry Ford failed and went broke five times before succeeding. What was his view on failure? He said, "Failure provides the opportunity to begin again, more intelligently." FW Woolworth, R. Macy, Albert Einstein, and Louis Pasteur all faced repeated failures in life only to achieve great things. Eric Hoffer writes, "Our achievements speak for themselves. What we have to keep track of are our failures, discouragements, and doubts. We tend to forget the past difficulties, the many false starts, and the painful groping. We see our past achievements as the end result of a clean forward thrust, and our present difficulties as signs of decline and decay." How true is that? We need to remember those trials to fully appreciate the richness of our success. Failing correctly is paramount to success.

When we get knocked down, in life our proper response is critical. When you get knocked down, you get up, dust yourself off, and move forward again. You don't start all over, and you don't quit. Let's say you are leaving a store and are walking across a parking lot when you stumble and fall. As you lay there, do you think, *I need to go back to the store and start my journey all over*, that would be stupid. It would be just as stupid to lay there thinking how badly you failed to walk across the lot, so you might as well lay there and give up.

Seasons change, snow falls, spring comes, and there you are, lying in the same spot. No, you get up, and move forward from the spot you fell. Likewise, where we fail in life is where we learn from that failure and move forward.

So when life gets you down, when you feel like a complete and utter failure, remember those who've gone before, who've set the bar on failure to heights we will probably never reach, and take heart. Failing is often the main prerequisite to success. As Robert F. Kennedy wrote, "Only those who dare to fail greatly can achieve greatly." Fail today—tomorrow may just be your heyday.

As a Christian, I sometimes I feel wholly inadequate in my Christian walk. Around others I can "be spiritual," I can talk the talk and walk the walk, even if I don't feel it; in fact, I've learned that every facet of the Christian life can be faked, if you will, except one—prayer. Everything else is basically a man-to-man experience, but prayer is man to God, and I just can't fool God. When I pray, my heart has to be right, my self has to be totally and completely honest, for He knows the truth anyway.

So I tell Him, I just don't feel worthy, I just don't feel spiritual all the time, and I often feel inadequate. And He reminds me that I am not worthy, that I am saved through His grace, His love, and His mercy. I'm not called to be "spiritual," but to be honest, transparent, and true to His message, for I am not the message, I'm just the messenger. As for feelings of inadequacy, He reminds me of some of those giants in our faith:

Abraham and Sarah, considered themselves too old,
Noah, who had a drinking problem,
Isaac the daydreamer,
Jacob the liar,
Rahab the prostitute,
David, who had an affair and had the husband murdered,
Elijah, who was suicidal,
Jonah, who ran from God,

Peter, a common fisherman who denied Christ,
Moses with his speech problems,
Joseph, the abused,
Martha the worrier,
Zacchaeus, who was too small,
Paul, the persecutor and persecuted,
The multi-divorced Samaritan woman,
    or John the Baptist, the bug-eater, and He reminds me that it isn't what I can do for Him that matters, it's what He can do through me if I only make myself available.

Three-Word Phrases

O nce, I was pondering the impact of three little words. A small phrase that causes a huge impact on a relationship when it occurred to me that there are a number of three-word phrases, what I like to call "Relationship Enrichers," that when properly and frequently used can really boost our relationships. Now, saying three little words may not seem difficult, but some phrases for some people may take some real practice. But, for now, try some of these and see what happens.

I was wrong.

You go first.

I miss you.

May I help?

I am sorry.

Thank-you for____.

I appreciate you.

You're the best.

Please help me.

Simple phrases, surely, but packed with power. Relationship enrichers.

But the most powerful of all the simple phrases, the most incredibly impactful one is simply, "I Love You."

Tithing versus Giving

I truly believe that deep down, if only we could be completely honest with ourselves, the majority of Christians have issues with tithing. I say that because the majority of Christians fail to tithe on a regular basis. I think it stems from several wellsprings. The first is insecurity, for in today's world, more and more families are living paycheck to paycheck, barely making ends meet, and it takes faith to set aside a tithe for God's work. They haven't experienced enough of God's grace to trust that He'll do exactly what He promises and meet their needs. Much of this stems from their inability to completely trust Him in all areas of their life, not just finances. You see, it's much easier to tithe when you see God working in other areas of your life as well.

When I was a teenager I read a little book, hardly more than a pamphlet, called, *My Heart, God's Home*. It described our heart like a house, and when we first let God in, He enters into our living room. We've turned that over to Him now. Next, we give Him another area of our lives, and now He owns the kitchen. This goes on throughout the rooms of the house, and the more we relinquish our lives to God, the more in control of our heart, His house, He is. But then, the book talks about this one little room, a closet really, just a small space we hang onto for our own. We just fight to hang onto it, whether it be finances, drinking, smoking, pornography, swearing, or pride—it doesn't matter what the vice, what matters is we refuse to give it up. And as long as we hang onto it, we restrict the work of the Holy Spirit in our lives. I share this story because that little closet could be what causes your resentment to giving.

A second wellspring that hinders our tithing is how the church in general teaches the principle of tithing. Paul lays out the principle of giving, not tithing, in 2 Corinthians 9:6–8 when he says, "He who sows sparingly will also reap sparingly, and he who sows bountifully will also reap bountifully. So let each one give as he purposes in his heart, not grudgingly or of necessity, for God loves a cheerful giver. And God is able to make all grace abound toward you, that you, always having all sufficiency in all things, may have an abundance for every good work."

Way back in Genesis, we see another principle of pleasing God through our giving and that is from the example of Abel. Cain grew crops and brought some as an offering to God. Abel was a shepherd, and likewise brought an offering, but his was the firstborn of his flock. God honored his offering, but Cain's not so much. The reason why Abel drew God's favor was because he chose to honor God with his firstborn, placing God before anything else.

So looking at these two principles, taken right out of the Bible, we see we should honor God first with our giving; and second, it should be what we can give cheerfully. So where did this ten percent rule come in that churches teach? We need to look at the context of the day to understand this "tithe" principle. The Children of Israel had escaped Egypt after some four hundred years of captivity, crossed the wilderness, and were now conquering the Promised Land. Each tribe of Israel was given a designated area of land to spread out and populate, that is all tribes but Levi's, for the Levites were the priests of the nation.

So God commanded that each of the other eleven tribes allow for a city for the Levites in their land, and to furnish that city with ten percent of their crops and flocks for the welfare of the priests living in their land and serving them. What we see then is tithing was under the Law of Moses; and as believers, we are no longer under that law. Further, the Old Testament tithe was actually an involuntary tax to support Israel, specifically the Levites, but also widows and orphans. Tithing is not mentioned anywhere in the New Testament, especially not found in the instructions to the Churches, but much is said about giving.

Generous grace is the teaching of the New Testament. I do believe it is important to give intentionally, not randomly or sporadically, if we indeed want to experience God's bountiful blessings. There are many verses that talk about giving and about the condition of the heart when we give, and that is so important. But we are not, nor should not be bound by a set rule of ten percent. First, as we learn to intentionally give what we purpose in our hear we can afford, and do so cheerfully, God will bless us. As we prosper, it is easy to give more to Him who is blessing us, and He blesses us further. I know many dedicated Christians who give far more than ten percent of their income, and God just continues to financially bless them. His shovel is so much bigger than ours, and we will never be able to out give Him! I can tell you from a personal perspective that I remember my parents giving all my life. And I don't remember a time that God didn't provide above and beyond their expectations.

There was a time when my dad stepped out in faith and quit his "regular" job at a local company to go into selling cars full time. He had always dabbled in cars, but this was really his dream job. It was the only time in my life that I remember seeing my dad unsure, and it shook me a little. I remember I was a young newlywed and going away to college at this time; and just before leaving, I was in his new office with him. I remember him telling me he had to sell at least two good cars a month to make his bills and stuff, and I'd never seen him worried like that. A couple months later, I was home visiting and was sitting in his office. I asked him how business was, and he said, "Business stinks. I've only sold seven cars this week." Seven cars that week! A couple months ago, he was hoping for two a month. God indeed blessed him bountifully.

So we need to give intentionally and cheerfully. We also need to give it out of our first fruits. We don't tell God let me see what's left and I'll give, we give to God and tell cable I'll see if I can afford you next month. God deserves our best. After all, He gave us His best and one hundred percent. Jesus sacrificed everything for us. Aren't we lucky God didn't stop giving at ten percent? We are stewards of what God has given us; so, in reality, we are returning to God what is already His. We give from the heart, grateful for what we've been entrusted with. Jesus told the parable of the three men who were given charge of money for their boss. One buried it so it would be safe, one made a little off his, and one made a good return off his. The man who buried his was punished, and his lot given to the guy who did well. The moral is that God wants us to use what we're given and return to Him out of our bounty. It springs from an inner desire to please our God.

Pastors don't like this mind-set because they make their living off the giving of their people. Some pastors just can't let go of the finances though. I went to a church, a large church, some years ago, and we outgrew our facility. We had bought some land and were studying the costs and plans to build, but clearly we needed somewhere to house our growth while things were built. Someone saw an anchor store had closed down in the center of a shopping mall, and we pursued whether that space was available to rent in the interim. I won't go into the whole long story, but the ending was we bought the whole mall, which wasn't for sale, we got more financing approved than we needed for the purchase, remodel, and move. We sold the land we were going to use to expand at a profit, and we sold our old building and got a down payment on it that covered all our moving costs. God's hand was clearly on it from beginning to end.

After we were moved in and all set up, the leadership began a monthlong series on giving over and above, giving until it hurt financially, to cover our building program, and even made a DVD to share in small groups throughout the weeks to come. I was in a meeting where they (the leadership) was really pushing us, small group leaders, to "step up and be an example" to our group to get everyone to commit and sign pledge cards. I said to them, "Why don't you just tell the people one time what you need, then trust God to work in their hearts? Clearly, God's hand has been on this whole ordeal."

I'll never forget the response. "No, Bud, you don't understand how this works. We have to keep pounding it in to get everyone on board."

I don't know how it works? I thought we trust God, ask the people, and let God work like He had been doing all along. It was at this point I realized that some of our pastors didn't understand how God works.

I also believe we are to give outside the local church. Before retiring as a small business owner, I frequently helped out our local Crisis Pregnancy Center, our Salvation Army, our Goodwill, our food pantry, and several other local organizations that helped the homeless or the needy. Sometimes, my help to these came at the expense of my local church, but it was where I believed God wanted me to give. We can give more than financially also. I often used my company truck and men to haul things for our local organizations, or donated furniture, bought boots and socks, cases of diapers, and toilet paper. Giving doesn't always mean money. God blesses our time and other resources when we use them to honor Him and help others.

Understanding Loneliness

For a good portion of the last couple decades, I've been alone, or rather, outside the bounds of a romantic relationship. I've never really been alone, for I have my relationship with Jesus. Yet, on occasion, when I start to feel down, the memories tend to remind me being alone isn't as bad as being with the wrong person. After all, that's the lesson learned, it is better to be alone than to be in the wrong relationship. I know that goes against societal wisdom, which seems to push us into relationships whether we're ready or not, and often before we know if we even like the other.

I remember some years ago when my folks moved into a new condo not far from my home. I made it a habit of dropping in three to four times a week to check on them, help out if needed, etc. Occasionally, we have a meal together. I think they really enjoyed my company, not just as a son, but as a person, for I meet in each of them a different need and a different desire. I remember Mom once saying, "We're sure glad you don't have anyone in your life right now. It makes more time for us."

I've teased her about praying for me and my relational status, for she is ever vigilant about praying for the right person for me, but I told her I now understand what she's praying for—no woman so I can spend time with them! We laughed, but usually in jest there is underlying truth, if we choose to seek it out. This truth—I'm extremely lucky to have both parents still living and active at my age and theirs, and those were precious memories we were making for those times when we won't have each other. I'm glad I could recognize the importance of each visit. I pray that my kids, that all those I care about, will realize sooner, rather than later or too late, the importance of family and relationships (not that they don't know now necessarily, but everyone's so busy that sometimes relationships are sacrificed for more "important things" like work, sports, commitments, etc.).

Sometimes, I miss having a hand to hold, eyes to gaze into, lips to kiss, and a person to love. I miss companionship. But, I don't miss drama, anger, or unrealized expectations. I don't miss the unrelenting pain of being betrayed no matter what the form. I don't miss the hurt, the agony when my vulnerability is violated. I watch movies now; and if I get emotional at a well-played drama, I am not ridiculed for my emotions, for I am alone. I can be completely me, free and easy, with no one or no desire to impress. I don't hurt my feelings, I don't forget important dates, and I am not insensitive to myself. Sometimes, I let myself down, but I'm forgiving of myself, for I know how flawed and broken I am. But I don't have someone with which to share, someone to laugh with, to cry with, to snuggle in the cold, to chase on the beach for I am alone. The scales swing back and forth.

It's important to realize that being alone is different than being lonely. Society teaches that those who are alone are probably lonely. But I beg to differ. One can be in the middle of a thousand people, be in the midst of a relationship, and be completely lonely while never being alone. Lonely is unmet needs, lonely is unrealized desire. Lonely is recognizing the hole in one's heart and not knowing how to fill it. That happens when relationships are wanting. Alone is not lonely. While occasionally I feel lonely, the feeling passes, for I am never alone. While most of my relationships may have been flawed or failed, I have one that never fails me, no matter how often I fail it. It is my relationship with Jesus Christ. He never lets me down. With Him, I can be completely alone in the eyes of the world, but never lonely.

Vulnerability and Mercy

Vulnerability and mercy; I wonder if we really understand these attributes of God. The Bible talks of God's mercy and also of Jesus's vulnerability. Yet they are at opposite ends of the spectrum.

Mercy flows from a position strength. God is a god of mercy because he operates from a position of strength. He is all-powerful, all-knowing, all-seeing, and can't operate from anywhere except strength. He is the Uncreated, and we are His created; and no matter how big, strong, or smart we think, we are we can never match His strength or wisdom.

Jesus, on the other hand, lived vulnerability. Being vulnerable is living from a position of weakness. Yet, the dichotomy is that Jesus, the Son of the Almighty God, with all the attributes of God, set aside his deity and donned the cloak of humanity, the cloak of vulnerability. Jesus chose to become vulnerable, and he instructed us, as his followers, to do the same.

Vulnerability means purposely exposing ourselves, our weaknesses, to allow others to know us in our weakness, for it is in our weakness that we can find strength. It sounds like a conundrum, but in reality, it is the secret to living a Christ-centered life. In or own strength, our basic carnal instinct is to hide our weaknesses and deal with our world from our strengths. The problem with that approach is that there is always someone stronger, smarter, or bigger than us, and they aren't afraid to knock us down a few pegs. It is the Law of the jungle, the instinct born of sin.

Vulnerability, however, says to the world to look at us, to see we are transparent and authentic; we are flawed and open about it. It asks the world to be accepting of us for who we are, not who we want or pretend to be. We must trust that our weaknesses won't be embraced and used against us. We must trust.

Being open and vulnerable can be the hardest thing for us to do, for our basic instinct is to protect ourselves, not leave ourselves open to potential hurt. Yet, when we do open ourselves, when we choose to follow Jesus's example, we are opening ourselves to God's mercy, to his forgiveness, and His love. And when we allow ourselves to be open and authentic before God, when we make ourselves vulnerable to Him, it allows God to flow and work through us. Satan, and evil, may have power on this earth for a time, but when we humble ourselves before God, we have the authority, His authority, to conquer whatever befalls our path. Understand, we are still weak and flawed creatures, but we command the power of the Uncreated through His Holy Spirit He has promised to everyone who believes and accepts Him.

A general in the army is just one man. Alone he cannot win a war or even fight a battle against a stronger larger foe with any hope of winning. He is neither big enough, nor strong enough. But the one thing he does have is authority. He can command soldiers to fight his battles. It is not through his strength that the battle is won, but through his authority. Likewise, God gives us the authority to command his power.

Vulnerability and mercy; mercy through vulnerability; strength through weakness; understanding these traits and their relationship to each other will help us lead a richer life.

Where Does God Come From?

I am often amazed at how our finite minds try to tackle infinite concepts. God, in His very nature, is infinite; and we are unable to even begin to comprehend Him aside from those attributes that He chooses to share with us through his word, the Bible. Yet, people still ask questions like, "If God can do anything then can He make a rock so heavy that He can't lift it?" And the answer, of course, is yes. My God, the Infinite Creator of our universe, can certainly do something so mundane. Don't ask me how for my finite mind cannot grasp it, but because He can do anything then that is certainly within the scope of His power. We live on a continuum, and thus are bound by time, space, and matter. These things define our existence. God, however, is not bound by any of these things, for He exists outside our continuum and indeed created them. He is not bound by them, and if He were, he would be finite also and certainly not worthy of our worship. It is the what, when, and where God created the continuum that defines our existence. The what (matter), the when (time), and the where (space) are all found in God's trilogy of trilogies

Let's look at the very first words God gave us in His Word. The first ten words of Genesis chapter one read, "In the beginning God created the heavens and the earth." When? In the beginning, the start of time, this consists of past, present, and future—one trilogy. Where? The heavens, which is defined by specific length, and depth, and width—the second trilogy. And what? The earth, consisting of solids, liquids, and gases—God's third trilogy.

As creator, God is clearly outside theses boundaries that He created, much like parents are outside the boundaries they create for their children. Children may not understand their boundaries, and often test them, but a good parent knows they are there for the protection and well-being of the child. In the exact same way, our Heavenly Father does not explain all to us, but we can rest in the assurance that He has only our best interests at heart. If we could explain God, then there would be no mystery to Him, no reason for our adoration and worship. Someday, for those who believe in Him and call His Son Jesus Christ their Lord and Savior, someday, the Apostle Paul tells us we will know fully, even as we are fully known. Now, we see in part and prophesy in part, but one day, we shall see clearly and understand fully this Infinite Creator, but only after the shackles have been removed from our finite minds.

My response to those who try to think up paradoxes and contradictory puzzles and statements to try and trip up believers, I say to you this, try and picture in your mind complete nothingness, the total absence of everything. If you can do that, I can answer any and all questions you have pertaining to God. (However, it is impossible, for even a vacuum is "something," a void is still space). You see, absolute nothingness is an infinite concept, one which our finite brains try to understand but can only come up lacking, for we are shacked by our finite limitations, So, one day, when God has healed this broken creation and believers share in eternity with the Uncreated, we will have our answers. Until then, God comes from that which no man can understand, perhaps from that absolute nothingness, before the constraints of time and forever more to be.

X-amine Your Zeal!

It's time to do a reality check. Are you living life, day-to-day, stuck in the same old rut, nothing exciting, nothing new? It's time to break free from that lifestyle. It starts out comfortable because it's known, but soon, it becomes drab and confining. We become chained to dull and secure when we are promised abundant and fulfilling! But we must step outside our comfort zone. We aren't promised a smooth easy life; rather, Jesus says we will encounter trials, but He came to give us abundant life despite facing trials.

Here's a tip for you, Satan is alive and well on this earth, and he likes nothing better than tepid Christians. You know the type, their face might crack if they broke into a smile, they go to church Sunday, and do nothing except work and eat and sleep the rest of the week. Satan's perfect Christian, and he's more than willing to leave them alone as long as they don't make waves. But look out for that wave-making Christian, for Satan is all over him, trying to hinder him and trip him up. And Jesus is there bolstering and strengthening him during his trials! Life is rich, exciting, and sometimes difficult, but exciting when we purpose to live intentionally for Jesus! And here's your second tip, the outcome is already determined, and you know what? God wins, and Satan loses—big time and forever. There are only two sides in this fight, either you are for Jesus, or you are against Him. There are no other options, no other choices. If you fail to accept Him, then you are against him, and your team loses. If you are for Him, you can have an exciting abundant life. If you are against Him, you can expect a humdrum unfulfilled life on this earth, but your eternity will be popping!

Fire, brimstone, worms, and decay—it's no Club Med, but it's all yours for eternity.

So, it's time to evaluate this life, is it worth living intentionally, getting the most out of our days, or are you happy just living a default life? The choice is yours and yours alone, but know that many are praying you make the right choice. If you do, look me up in heaven—I'll be the eternally grateful one!

About the Author

D ale "Bud" Brauer is a retired businessman and small business owner from the Northern Illinois area now making his home in Ridge Manor, Florida. Bud is the father of three children, two sons and a daughter, and six grandkids.

After graduating Judson College (now Judson University) with a degree in Human Relations (psychology and sociology), Bud entered the workforce, running a small business, which he eventually owned. After more than thirty years of practical experience to add to his educational experience, Bud has a well of experience to draw upon. He believes that we learn more from our failures than our successes, and it is important to not only learn but learn not to repeat. In 2007, he began blogging and has over twenty-three thousand readers (Thoughts-Outside-the-Box. Blogspot.com) who enjoy his practical insights, common sense, biblical insights, and a fair dose of humor. After successfully blogging a number of years, Bud's daughter encouraged him to write a book, which he decided to do after retiring.

Since retiring, Bud does some business consulting as well as writing. This is his first book, but a second is in the works. Bud is also engaged in his local church, New Walk Community Church, in Zephyrhills, Florida.

You can follow him on Facebook at Facebook/bud.brauer

CPSIA information can be obtained
at www.ICGtesting.com
Printed in the USA
FFOW02n2031140318
45594099-46384FF